THE CREATIVE LEAP

Psychological Transformation Through Crisis

THE CREATIVE LEAP

Psychological Transformation Through Crisis

Verena Kast

translated by
Douglas Whitcher

Chiron Publications • Wilmette, Illinois

Originally published in 1987 as *Der schopferische Sprung: Vom therapeutischen Umgang mit Krisen*. Copyright 1987, Walter-Verlag AG, Olten.

Translation © 1990 by Chiron Publications

Library of Congress Catalog Card Number: 90-36345

Printed in the United States of America.
Edited by Siobhan Drummond Granner.
Book design by Nancy R. Snyder.

Library of Congress Cataloging-in-Publication Data:
Kast, Verena, 1943–
    [Schöpferische Sprung. English]
    The creative leap : psychological transformation through crisis /
Verena Kast ; translated by Douglas Whitcher.
        p.   cm.
    Translation of: Die schöpferische Sprung.
    Includes bibliographical references.
    ISBN 0-933029-32-2 : $14.95
    1. Crisis intervention (Psychiatry)—Case studies. 2. Stress
(Psychology)—Case studies. 3. Anxiety—Case studies. I. Title.
RC480.6.K3713   1991
155.9—dc20   90-36345
                                                          CIP

ISBN 0-933029-32-2

Cover photograph by Kurt Hasselquist.

Contents

Preface to English Edition

I am delighted that this book, which has met with such a receptive German-speaking audience, could be translated into English and published by Chiron. I hope I am also able to reach my American readers.

Here I would like to offer my sincere thanks to Douglas Whitcher, who translated my German manuscript with great interest, empathy, and knowledge of the field; to Elizabeth Burr, who was consulted on the translation and carefully edited it; and to Murray Stein, who brought the whole project into motion.

Verena Kast

Preface to First Edition

The theme of crisis and crisis intervention has concerned and fascinated me for some time.

I first presented my experiences with what appear to me as typical crises, along with their accompanying interventions, at the Lindauer Therapy Week. Then, in a somewhat expanded version which forms the basis of the present book, I lectured on "The Meaning of Crisis Intervention in the Therapeutic Process" at the University of Zürich during the summer semester of 1986.

Here I would like to gratefully acknowledge the generous, warm interest with which my remarks were received, as well as the many suggestions I have been given.

My deepest gratitude goes to all of those who have allowed me to reproduce excerpts from our crisis interventions, in part verbatim, to describe their crises and the dynamics underlying them.

Very special thanks are due to Christa Henzler, who worked through the jungle of my manuscript with technical skill and admirable patience.

Verena Kast

Introductory Remarks

This book deals with the possibility and practical execution of crisis intervention in psychotherapeutic practice. It focuses on a special form of crisis intervention, which is to be distinguished from that practiced in crisis-intervention centers.

People experiencing crises are usually referred to a therapist, sometimes by the attending physician, but in many cases by the pastor. Crises can also arise in the context of therapeutic processes already under way, which become the occasion for crisis interventions. In a psychotherapeutic practice, we generally have more to do with veiled crises, where the term "crisis" in a narrow sense no longer applies. These crises are not dramatically apparent, but may manifest themselves in ongoing problem situations such as inexplicable fatigue, loss of desire, or psychosomatic complaints.

Although crisis intervention is not the daily bread of my own practice, I feel I have something to contribute on the subject.

By means of clinical vignettes, I will be portraying typical life situations that can precipitate crises as well as the psychodynamics that characterize them. Naturally each crisis is unique, and yet from an overall perspective we can distinguish, for instance, between a crisis of loss in the strict sense and a suicidal crisis.

My aim is to describe the typical psychic processes in the background of these crises, as well as the developmental possibilities contained in them.

At the same time, it seems extraordinarily important to me to include in my reflections the feelings that we therapists have in the face of these crises. To begin with, someone in a crisis triggers quite specific "crisis feelings" in us as fellow human beings: either we are infected by their feelings of panic, or else we are totally focused and present for them, sensing that we are in a situation which could "make all the difference." Or then again we fend the crisis off by trivializing it or in some other way. How we respond to a given crisis depends on the attitudes we have developed in our lives toward crisis in general. How crisis-friendly are we, how tolerant, how allergic to crisis? It also depends on what kinds of fears and threats are called up in our psyches by different kinds of crises, and on how we have learned to deal with our anxieties.

We will see that there are fairly typical reactions to certain crises, reactions that are common to many; perhaps we could call these reactions collective forms of counter-transference. In addition, we have our own personal reactions to individual crises,

1

reactions which may be decisive for the success or failure of a crisis intervention, determining our methods of approaching it.

I consider these countertransference feelings, as I call them here, an integral aspect of crisis intervention.

By countertransference, I understand first and foremost an analyst's feelings in relation to an analysand going through a crisis, feelings that the analyst does not allow to slip away but holds onto in some form.[1] These feelings of the analyst may correspond precisely to the feelings of the analysand, thus representing direct access to— or empathic understanding of—a person in a crisis. More often, we experience a defensive barrier in ourselves against feelings awakened in us by the analysand. By empathically taking note of such defenses, we can get a sense of the threat to which we feel subjected; it is usually the same one as the threat hanging over the individual in crisis or the analysand.[2]

But it is not only emotions that we experience in countertransference. Often we have the impression of being virtually dragged by a compulsive pattern of behavior into a particular role or relational pattern against our better judgment. Perhaps we speak of the analysand or person in crisis trying to manipulate us. As Sandler repeatedly points out, this attempt to manipulate represents an effort to remobilize a relational pattern which was once important because it offered security, and which now again offers the security needed to cope with an extraordinarily alarming life situation, where security matters above all else.[3]

It is essential to grasp the implications of these aspects of countertransference. First, the unconscious of the analysand communicates with that of the analyst;[4] second, one's unconscious is infected by the emotions of another person, especially in crisis situations, which are determined by strong emotions; and finally, this infection must be dealt with.

The third main objective of this book will be to demonstrate how such crisis situations, pervaded with intense anxiety, can be handled therapeutically. In order to make my method comprehensible, I have frequently cited verbatim interventions, sequences of dialogue transcribed from tapes (translated from Swiss German into High German by the author, and then into English by the translator). My aim is to present the reader not with "model interventions," but rather with factual interventions as I have conducted them in various therapeutic situations. I include them here in order to provide the most down-to-earth glimpse possible into therapeutic proceedings, well aware that there are aspects of the therapeutic process which elude all verbal representation.

Chapter 1

Crisis as Opportunity

We know that crises are also chances, opportunities for the greater unfolding of the personality, assuming that we limit ourselves here to those, among the many possible kinds of human crises, in the personal realm. Equipped with this perspective—crisis as opportunity—we can try to help those undergoing a crisis see the value of their situation. But at the same time, we can delude ourselves if we overlook the fact that the chances in many crises are not, and cannot be, taken advantage of.

A crisis can lead to a new experience of identity. We can emerge from a crisis with new behavioral possibilities, new dimensions of self-experience, and new ways of experiencing the world, maybe even with a new perception of meaning. A crisis can make us more competent in dealing with life, helping us overcome the feeling of being subjected to it. Whether any of these opportunities are actualized depends on whether we are able to see the crisis as a life situation in which the fate of existentially important matters is decided, or whether we see the crisis simply as an annoying but unessential accident to be forgotten as quickly as possible. The knowledge that every crisis can bring about one of many possible basic transformations is crucial. But whether we can perceive and grasp the personal, social, behavioral, and existential possibilities presented to us in a crisis depends further on whether we can come into real contact with our crisis. Intervening in a crisis means, in the first place, getting in touch with the crisis. But even then the crisis may still overpower us. It may even lead to a breakdown.

Types of Crises

Each of us is constantly faced with new problems in life. At first we attempt to get hold of and solve them by means of "old" categories of experience and problem-solving strategies that we have learned and to which we are accustomed. As we advance in years, new problems present themselves. The *developmental crises*, from puberty to old age, play themselves out rather dramatically. We might also think of crises arising from demands that at the moment exceed our powers. We usually suppose that these demands come at us from the outside, for example, the demands posed by our profession or family, by unemployment, change of residence, or retirement. All demands are not, however, pressures imposed from without. Externally imposed de-

3

mands can become stressful and overdemanding because we demand too much of ourselves in reaction to them. It goes without saying that *crises of demand* are to be seen against the background of social developments and threats at large. Finally, *crises of loss* are experienced in a variety of forms: losses through death, separation, changes in one's body, sickness, and old age; nor should one reckon lightly with the loss of work.

It is not easy to distinguish among crises arising from these various circumstances, but this is not as necessary as it may at first seem. Behind many crises of demand a developmental crisis lies hidden. Thus, we may feel quite threatened by a certain demand just because we have not yet completed some long-overdue step in our personal growth. The present crisis compels us to make up for the missing step as best we can. Many demands leading to a crisis are related to loss in one form or another. If, for example, we have lost our usual sense of well-being, a demand that, under normal circumstances, would challenge us to make our best effort, even giving us great satisfaction, may be too much for us.

In speaking of certain categories of crisis, I wish above all to indicate that the precipitating event of a crisis—whether a heightened demand or a serious loss—may not yet tell us what decisive life issue will be found at the root of the crisis in the final analysis. To get at this, we must ask what fundamental life problem and corresponding developmental impulse lie beneath the surface of a crisis.

Characteristics of Crisis

We speak of a crisis when an individual experiences a disconcerting disequilibrium between the subjective importance of a problem and the resources available for coping with it. In a crisis one's identity is threatened, and one's capacity for autonomy and free choice is called into question. When our capacity to choose and act freely is threatened, we respond with intense anxiety, for this capacity represents one of our highest values. Our anxiety, which may or may not be expresssed directly, lames us yet further. A sense of struggling in vain, combined with a growing level of anxiety, sooner or later forces us to surrender all the familiar strategies we had previously deployed. Nothing remains but to hope for a new inspiration, impulse, or idea. This might consist of a reformulation of the problem itself. To achieve a redefinition of the requirements for coping with the problem already constitutes a creative process. One has given up the old, useless strategies of behavior and coping in order to discover a new, more adequate notion for dealing with the problem at hand.

But even a whole new approach may not make the problem go away. Or we may not be able to concede a position of temporary powerlessness. We may not have the patience to wait for inspiration. All of these possibilities may occur in the face of the intense anxiety associated with crisis. Fear then increasingly takes the upper hand. Panic siezes one's entire personality and possesses one's existence. Here crisis intervention will probably be needed in one form or another. We may be lucky enough to encounter the right person in the right place saying or doing the right thing. Or a dream may appear to point the way to a new solution. But it is likely that the assistance of a crisis-intervention center or a therapist will now be required.

Intervention consists of a third party coming between an individual and that individual's crisis. The mediator puts distance between them, freeing the individual enough so that he or she can get into contact with the crisis. With the crisis situation "held off" to some extent, better access can be gained to the possibilities lying hidden within it.

Most simply, crisis denotes separation, quarrel, decision, verdict. The crisis marks the high point of an event, but also its turning or shifting point. When we speak of crisis in this sense we are referring to a particular phase of transformation implied in the expression "coming to a head." A psychic transformation, like a storm, gathers on the horizon. The variety of contexts in which the word "crisis" is used can easily lead us to conclude that anything living can undergo a crisis. Crises are experienced as occasions of urgency: in the unrelenting grip of a crisis, panic siezes the individual. No longer able to think of a way out, he or she seems to be blind and deaf to anything but his or her problem and how to solve it. One feels utterly helpless and is convinced that nothing will ever change—at least not for the better. Often the following image is expressed: "I feel as if I were in a dark tunnel. I don't see any way out." This no-exit tunnel generates panic, and the crisis invades one's entire existence, sparing nothing. Without being able to think of or see anything else, one's being is radically narrowed down to the object of the crisis, and one's concern extends no further than the boundaries of one's own existence.

To get a more concrete idea of the nature of crisis, we can begin by reflecting on how we react to small, everyday crises. Let us say we have to be on time at an unknown place to give a lecture. We take the car, and although we have allowed a generous amount of time, during the drive the time melts into thin air, and a thunderstorm or snowstorm is added to the picture. We lose our way, and at a certain point, we can no longer keep the thought at bay that we will never be able to arrive on time. Anxiety takes over; perhaps we behave even more hectically, or perhaps we simply freeze. Defying reality, we attempt the impossible with the result that our destination becomes even more difficult to find, and we become even more lost. Usually our own crisis intervention comes into play at some point; we take a deep breath, maybe even stop and say to ourselves, "At least I am still alive! Yes, it is extremely embarrassing to arrive late, but it is better than not arriving at all." Then calm can return; we can contemplate what is to be done in order to rescue the situation.

The crisis intervention in this case consists of replacing one value with another. The values of punctuality and reliability are no longer put in first place, but rather the supraordinate value of still being alive. Even such a small and commonplace crisis demonstrates quite clearly the extent to which anxiety is involved. To just this extent, crisis intervention must consist of guidance in coping with anxiety. Since fear is our reaction to one of our values being threatened, replacing a less important value with a higher, more comprehensive value is a way of coping with anxiety. If an individual's highest value is threatened, there is clearly no replacing it. The anxiety level of crises involving the loss of life goes off the scale.

It hardly needs to be said that many crises are not resolved through the intervention of some center or therapist, but rather by talking with another person. A taxicab driver or a waiter may sing an astonishingly appropriate song. When we feel a crisis coming to a head, we often talk with someone who can still see more possibilities than we can, who can thus put us at ease and help us to refocus on new perspectives. Then it often turns out that the crisis never really reaches its peak. This brings up another essential aspect of crisis: many persons become incapable of speaking with others in the thick of their crises. Often they undergo a simultaneous crisis in their relationships as well. They may have no desire to ask anyone else to listen even once to their problems. Or they may have lost their faith—if they ever had it—that opening up emotionally to another human being might open up their own life difficulties.

To qualify as a crisis, the disturbance of equilibrium mentioned above must be:

— serious,

— acute, and

— not to be coped with by employing the usual compensatory means.[1]

Such a crisis can strike persons who usually function well and are compatible with their surroundings, as well as those who have a more difficult time with themselves and their environment.

Times of crisis are times in a person's life marked by a highly restricted intensity. They are situations of birth. It goes without saying that such situations cannot sustain intense anxiety and stress over extended periods of time. A crisis can subside, or it can become chronic. It can precipitate disease and induce ongoing psychological problems—without the situation of urgency persisting. This gives crisis both its unpleasant character and its unique capacity for breakthrough. We find ourselves in a genuine borderline situation, without which no transformation is possible.

Crisis as a Turning Point

Crisis in the course of development means that moment in which the whole person suffers a reversal, and the individual emerges as a changed person armed with a new decision or sunk in defeat. The life history does not run an even chronological course but structures its time qualitatively, drives the development of experience to a peak where a decision has to be made. It is only by fighting against development that an individual can make the futile attempt of keeping himself at the point of decision without making one. Where he does this the decision is made for him by the factual progression of life. Every crisis has its time. It cannot be anticipated nor can it be evaded. Like everything in life it has to mature. It need not appear in acute form as a catastrophe but may take place quietly and inconspicuously, yet nevertheless be decisive for the future.[2]

This quotation from Jaspers contains another clear statement of the view that a crisis is the last passageway to a transformation and the last obstacle to change. Something in the life of an individual shifts, and suddenly many things become possible: a new experience of oneself and the emergence of a new identity; the chance to learn new problem-solving strategies and to resolve old problems. These are creative possibilities. But a crisis can just as well result in a relapse, for there is also the possibility of falling into a trap with no exit. There is even the possibility that the crisis will be resolved by means of a suicide attempt. Jasper's definition makes it clear that crises are necessary, that they signify chances for transformation and growth. Jaspers is an existential philosopher, hence the supreme importance he attributes to the moment of decision. Existential philosophy values crises highly and seeks them out because they offer the possibility of changing life by taking it into one's own hands. At the peak of a crisis, a decision can no longer be postponed; no choice remains but to choose. This is the very thing that is so impossible for persons seeking crisis intervention. Since they are rigid with fear, only by releasing the tension of anxiety can the energy they need to make the required decision be freed. But decision also invariably means taking the risk of making a mistake. While Jaspers so strongly emphasizes decision, I would like to say in contrast that one may with justification also decide initially to wait and see.

Besides, not all crises are centered primarily around a decision. And they do not always build steadily toward a crescendo. For example, in a crisis of mourning—a typical crisis—the loss of a loved one often results in a deep identity crisis. One's life as a whole undergoes a drastic upheaval. Not so quickly transcended, this upheaval brings on a crisis.

There are crises that grow out of the inhibition of a creative adaptation to life and its requirements. But there are also crises that are related to swift and profound changes with which we cannot immediately cope, needing first to learn to cope.

Crisis and Anxiety

Every disintegration of the familiar, and every emergence of a new order of things, is accompanied with anxiety.

Anxiety is bodily. It is no wonder that many persons in the midst of a crisis get ill and then suffer from the physical illness instead of the real crisis. The illness masks the crisis. The crisis, the factors that precipitated it, its meaning and the developmental possibilities lying within it, can only be reached with difficulty. This may afford a certain psychic relief, but the narrowness belonging to the crisis situation remains. Anxiety and exclusion from consciousness of everything but a single problem allow the crisis to develop its own autonomous laws. The crisis takes over completely. In addition, the acute problem becomes linked to every other problem that ever existed. Earlier conflicts are relived together with the emotions that had characterized those situations, especially panic. This is why every crisis intervention should, in the first place, put those who are gripped by a crisis into real inner contact with their crisis.

By helping them perceive and accept the various emotions associated with their crisis, or simply by giving them some perspective, we bring such persons into relationship with their crisis. In a crisis intervention, we try to come between the individual and his or her crisis so that he or she gains the distance necessary to take up a conscious relationship with the crisis. Intervention reduces panic and allows for the discovery of resources with which to solve the underlying problem. In the end, the goal of a crisis intervention must include a practical solution to a very pressing problem.

But to begin with, relief and relaxation of tension must be introduced into the mood of panic. The second step consists of verbalizing the main issue latent in the crisis. This issue holds the key to the meaning of the crisis. The actual crisis intervention consists of this opening up of the confined psychic space and the relaxation of tension. Simply being able to open up to, confide in, and rely on another person accounts for a large measure of relief. Several talks usually follow the actual crisis intervention, during which the main problem is more clearly formulated. The meaning of the crisis becomes evident, and practical coping strategies are tried out. The crisis intervention can now stand on its own. The client has the feeling that the crisis is over and no further assistance is required. He or she can follow up with short-term therapy, more intense therapy, or even analysis. Alleviation of tension is one goal of crisis intervention. Recognition of the psychodynamics in the background of typical crises so that we can also impart information to the person in crisis is another goal. Above all, the therapist must know what the issue is. If we see the issue at the heart of the crisis and understand the psychodynamics connected with it, then we are in a position to go ahead with an intervention (excluding crisis with a psychotic background). Without this understanding, we quickly get the feeling that we must make a referral, possibly to a psychiatric hospital.

Finally, the question of whether or not to begin a crisis intervention depends on the anxiety experienced by the therapist. The greater the anxiety triggered, the less likely it is that the therapist will be capable of carrying out a crisis intervention. This is so because our anxiety level is an indicator of how threatened we feel by a given therapeutic situation. We feel more certain of ourselves if we understand what problems are involved in a crisis and what the related psychodynamics are. However, I am not saying that confidence in the face of anxiety is to be recommended in every case of crisis intervention. Rather, I think we should empathically perceive our anxiety and then decide whether it is advisable to summon the courage needed to face and overcome an apparently surmountable obstacle, or whether we are simply asking too much of ourselves.

Crisis interventions confront us with a fundamental problem: the panic that has seized someone in a crisis is transferred into the situation where the intervention should take place and becomes contagious. It makes us feel as if everything must proceed very quickly, if not immediately. We feel compelled to understand everything and have it all solved before our client even begins to speak, an attitude which prevents anything at all from working. Anxiety inhibits; it will inhibit everyone concerned with the crisis intervention. The therapist contributes his or her own anxiety in the form of a feeling of powerlessness, a feeling that compensates for the expectation of a miraculous solution. This huge demand, placed by therapists on themselves, often leads to the premature proffering of advice. We try to take on too many problems all at once. For, in spite of our sense that things are really quite stuck, we know from our experience as therapists, who often perform crisis interventions, that the crisis makes many things possible, that crisis situations are situations of transformation.

But to begin at a basic level, persons in crisis come to us like children arriving on the doorstep of a helper who can and should take charge of the entire matter. This is the first hurdle. Every crisis intervention should in the end be help for the sake of self-help. It is quite important to accept the fact that someone is approaching us in the position of a child hoping to find a helpful adult, but it is the goal of crisis intervention to free up the adult within this child. He or she needs to be reminded of how many difficult situations have already been survived and even mastered. For therapists this means, as in all situations of panic, taking a deep breath, getting in touch with one's own anxiety, perceiving it and at the same time achieving some distance from it. If too much anxiety is present, other helpers should be called in or the person in crisis should be referred elsewhere.

Therapists must establish clear boundaries at the outset. They must limit their own panic-filled desire to do everything, plainly declare what they are and are not prepared to do, and unequivocally state how much time they want to spend on this crisis intervention and when they can be reached by telephone. They should have someone else to call on for further clarification if the case is very complicated. Therapists must also be well aware of the fact that every crisis touches on the themes of their own lives with extreme poignancy and intense emotionality. They should become aware of how they react to these themes.

When we panic, our defense mechanisms function considerably less well than usual. Defense mechanisms perform the task of holding our undesirable feelings, affects, and perceptions at a distance from consciousness, protecting us from conflicts. They are coping devices that help us deal with anxiety and maintain emotional equilibrium. In a crisis, these coping devices may become disabled; we generally lose command of a diversified system of defenses and must operate with a reduced spectrum of serviceable mechanisms. Conflicts can emerge with unusual clarity and confront us with unaccustomed immediacy, especially the conflict behind the crisis. This makes crisis an opportunity: not only are our conflicts and complexes freed from their usual maxtrix of defenses, but our strengths and potential for creativity are also more available in the crisis situation than they were before or will be afterward. Conflict-producing patterns of relationship introduce themselves during the first contact between therapist and client. Conflicts in the realm of self-esteem, well out of reach under normal circumstances, are readily grasped in a crisis; deep disappointments and grievances, as well as fixed attitudes emerge. These conflicts can be sensed, experienced, and worked on in the relationship between therapist and client in crisis. Often they are the deeper reason for the crisis.

Goals of Crisis Intervention

The goals of crisis intervention now become clear: first, to discover the precipitating event of the crisis within the context of the related psychodynamics and so to work out the deeper meaning of the crisis; second, to facilitate a new way of coping with anxiety; and third, to help in dealing with outer problems. Crisis intervention consists not only of psychotherapeutic, but also of instrumental help. Thought should be given to choosing social institutions which might assist with one or another aspect of the problem. I recall, for example, a man who had collected a never-ending supply of debts. A major reason why he staggered from crisis to crisis was that he could not get out from under his mountain of debts. Once a social agency had assumed management of his debts, organizing their repayment without taking away his share of the responsibility, we could turn our attention to his work crisis.

A crisis intervention also involves asking the basic question of what resources might still be available in a particular case, where sources of help might still exist for the person concerned. What areas of life remain relatively untouched by the crisis? Are there relationships that might carry some of the load? Is help coming from the unconscious? Often emerging precisely at the time of a crisis, helpful dreams are of particular importance. One often hears the fear voiced, in this connection, that bringing dreams into the process might confront the person in crisis with the unconscious too intensely. I do not share this fear in the least and believe that the most important question is how we deal with dreams in the crisis situation. Can we adopt them as help coming from the unconscious, and at the same time relate them to the concrete situation?

The actual crisis intervention is accomplished only if we can establish contact with the individuals and thereby understand the threat he or she feels. This represents a huge achievement. Persons coming to crisis interventions are not used to talking about their troubles. This may be the first time they experience how much sharing their problems can reduce pressure. Another point in establishing contact is to portray the crisis as an opportunity. But we mustn't forget to meet affected persons where they are, taking their regressive tendencies seriously, noting the degree of their regression, comforting them, and even breaking their fall. Nor can we afford to disregard practical sources of help. We may be called on to help in finding shelter and in making plans for where to go next. The point is to get the person in crisis to talk and to express various emotions. The therapist's function is to structure, order, and understand, but also to manage practical resources. What matters above all is for therapists to devote their empathic attention to the person in crisis—without, however, omitting the necessary "getting down to business"—that brings to fruition the delicate process of opening up to another human being.

Crisis and the Creative Process

In principle, I am of the view that crisis intervention can best orient itself according to a model of the creative process. The term "crisis" describes a very decisive moment in the creative process wherein we find ourselves so engaged because we can no longer solve a problem with known ways and means at a time when it matters a great deal to us that the problem be solved. (I am speaking here of creativity on the level of personality, not of art.)

Once we have made the problem that is vexing us conscious, the *phase of preparation* follows. During this phase we gather the relevant material and attempt to see the problem from different perspectives. We collect ideas about how others have dealt with the problem without yet drawing our own conclusions. At a certain point we have gathered enough ideas and notions to confuse ourselves. Sometimes we think we have discovered something; then again we feel as if we don't understand anything at all. This phase is accompanied by the feeling of tension.

After the phase of preparation comes the *phase of incubation,* during which the problem is processed in the unconscious. This is a restless, frustrating time. Solutions to the problem surface, only to be cast away again. The problem brings us under increasing pressure. Although we suspect that a solution is about to hatch, we nevertheless suffer from the feeling of being ineffective and incompetent. Worrying that all our efforts are futile, we begin to doubt that we are worth anything at all. The problem preoccupies us almost completely. But in spite of the apparent futility of it all, we retain the sense that something is happening, something which is just not within our grasp yet. In this phase we must abandon the desire to take the matter actively into our own hands. The phase of preparation represented an attempt to illuminate the problem from every angle with the greatest possible consciousness. The phase of incubation calls for "letting it happen" in the faith that a way to order the chaos will occur to us. The creative crisis is located in this phase of the creative process and corresponds to the situation in which persons undergoing crisis can find themselves. If they have faith that something will be achieved through their crises, that they must only actively wait to receive whatever signs the body and soul will give, then their crises remain bearable. But the anxiety that tends to predominate in a crisis pressures us into feeling that we must get hold of everything and organize it all, alone and as independently as possible. This is where crisis intervention comes in. The therapist brings to the situation the conviction that the problem can be resolved, and the client gladly takes this to heart in the hope that the crisis will be a rite of passage issuing in a transformation. Those who make interventions perceive the feelings associated with the crisis, thus helping to order them, accept them, and bear them. But intervenors also help the person in crisis comprehend the underlying problem by illuminating it with their knowledge, and become aware of emerging recognitions.

The flash of new recognition belongs to the next phase of the creative process, the *phase of insight.* A clear and significant recognition is achieved. One breathes a sigh of relief. The chaos has ordered itself. New recognitions coupled with new insights, new modes of experience, and personal behavior—these are the fruits born out of the crisis as a creative process.

In the creative process, following the phase of insight, which was accompanied by feelings of joy and relief, is the *phase of verification*. Here the arrived-at insight is given shape by concentration until it becomes communicable, until it can be precisely and concisely expressed, until one's concrete experience is congruent with a communicable finding. The creative insight can now be shared with others.

In the context of crisis intervention, this phase represents an attempt to clarify the change we have undergone in the process of coping with the crisis. This means communicating the change to others as much as it means grasping it ourselves. For a crisis intervention conducted within the framework of a psychotherapeutic practice, this is an important time to reappraise what was experienced at the turning point of the crisis. At this time we learn whether the crisis intervention was primarily a matter of easing tension—which is essential and not to be dismissed—or whether it also facilitated the discovery of new modes of experience, behavior, and relationship that can now be lived. Since an individual's entire existence is drawn into the crisis, comprehensive transformations can take place, which explains the enthusiasm we may have in the midst of a crisis. Crises are highly disturbing and filled with risk. They offer an opportunity for great change to occur in a single creative leap, which must, however, subsequently prove itself in confrontation with the environment. Many rivers find new riverbeds, only to be coerced by forces of circumstance back into their old ones.

I understand crisis intervention as a therapeutic procedure whose aim is to get into contact with the crisis, whose means is to open up and reach out to another person, and whose hope is to realize and actualize the radical and creative change embedded within the crisis. The conditions necessary for creativity are knowledge, skill, inner freedom, and a feeling of security.[3] Persons in the grip of a crisis may have none of these, which explains why they cannot deal creatively with the crisis. The state of being gripped by anxiety is what most clearly differentiates those who become stuck in a crisis from those who find a way to deal creatively with it. Hence the importance in crisis intervention of devoting great care to the management of anxiety. Only by learning to deal with our anxiety can we become creative.

In general terms, crisis intervention can be seen according to the model of the creative process. The tasks are to discern the precipitating problem as acutely as possible, to develop a plan for dealing with the problem, and to find and mobilize sources of relief from the environment. It is also essential to convey to the troubled person the notion that the crisis can open doors to creative resolutions. In my view, the most important thing is that therapists behave with the conviction that personal growth can subsume and transcend crisis in a great leap forward. This means more than trust in the potential creativity of upheaval, temporarily offered by the therapist; it also means giving priority to the perception of emotions and the dispersal of anxiety, as well as attending to expressions of the unconscious which are especially precise in

Figure 1.1
Phases in the Creative Process

Phase	**Accompanying Emotion**
1. Phase of Preparation	tension
• Assembling of information	
• Maximal intake—minimal categorization	
2. Phase of Incubation	uneasiness
	frustration
• Problem ferments inside—comes to a head	doubting one's self-worth and competence
Crisis Situation	inhibition
	anxiety
	"congestion"
3. Phase of Insight	joy
	relief
• Clear recognition—"Aha"	
4. Phase of Verification	concentration
• Insight is shaped, examined, tested	

crises. The last point can be illustrated by dreams that occur during the mourning process which virtually compel mourners to cope with their crises, deliberately introducing the steps necessary to master them. But it is also corroborated by the way in which the root conflict of a crisis constellates itself more boldly in the crisis-counseling situation than in other counseling situations, emerging during the first few minutes of the consultation.

Chapter 2

Crises of Maturation

By means of a brief example, I would like to clarify the essential characteristics of crisis intervention that I attempted to convey in the preceeding chapter.

A pastor called me. He was with a fifty-two-year-old man who was completely disoriented. He didn't think the man was psychotic, but found him quite unnerving, and asked me if I could make a crisis intervention. The pastor, having already attempted to speak with the man and calm him down, brought him to my office. The man requested that the pastor stay for our talk.

Seeming stoically self-possessed, this man did not actually give the impression of someone who easily gets into a crisis, but he was beside himself with rage and took no notice of anyone around him. At least, I did not feel that he took any notice of me. This was not immediately necessary, as his rage riveted me with all the force of a natural disaster.

He sat down. "Yes," he said, "just now, the entire way here, I have been talking about my anger. I feel like it's the end of the world. I can't stand it. My wife has this boyfriend. My anger is driving me crazy. I'm going to kill the guy. I'm going to kill my wife. I'm going to burn the place down. . . ." He continued on in this vein.

At some point he looked at me, then at the pastor, and said, "With a problem like this, you bring me to such a young lady?! As if anything could come of that!"

The pastor shrugged his shoulders. I said to the man, "I can understand your feeling that only a man could deal with your colossal rage, but let's give it a try anyway."

In this exchange we established contact with each other. I was hearing that a young lady could not deal with his problem, and yet I sensed that the emphasis was not so much on the theme of youth as it was on the theme of womanhood. My reply gave him the feeling that I understood his wish to share his anger with other men, while asking him to give us both a chance to solve his problem.

At first he began cursing again. One sensed this man's anxiety only indirectly, warded off by means of a boundless rage. Our initial encounter revealed that he couldn't control his anger very well, that he had a lot of fantasies about how he could act his anger out, and that, when angry, he became insensitive to those around him. Only after some time did he perceive that I was (in his eyes) a young woman, and I was already asking myself whether he was the type who doesn't think much of women—and how the feminine side within him fared. I asked him how he felt now.

14

He told me he could no longer sleep, he could no longer eat, he swung back and forth between being infuriated and being down in the dumps; yet he could still work. Then it came out that it had been only two days since he had learned about his wife's boyfriend. He portrayed his emotions quite dramatically.

The point of this crisis intervention would not be to unearth his emotions with painstaking care, but rather to prevent his emotions from completely swamping him. He had also indicated that in the realm of work—he was self-employed—he was still very much "his own man."

Here we are looking at a man caught in a crisis, for whom this was a rare occurrence, a man who could usually take quite a lot. He was also known to be a man who occasionally had serious, if short, temper tantrums. Continuing to describe his crisis, he said he was confused, had no idea what to do, thought it just could not be; surely he would wake up to find that it had only been a bad dream; nothing like this had ever happened in all his life. I asked him what it would really mean if his wife *did* have a boyfriend (I did not yet know nor had I asked exactly what sort of friendship it was). For him, the fact that his wife had a boyfriend could mean none other than: "She is leaving me. I will grow old. Nobody to look after me anymore. I'll dry up. Nobody to talk to anymore."

He was quite amazed at his own utterance, at his own fantasy. Now we begin to see that, while there was an outer event that had precipitated the crisis reaction, this event belonged, as usual, within a more comprehensive context. The precipitating event— coming from the outside—was the discovery that his wife had a boyfriend. This apparently became the event of a crisis because it became mixed up with the problem of getting old which he had repressed. Thus one suspects that what he was really putting up such a fight against was a crisis of maturation. His complaint to the pastor about being taken to such a young lady with his problem already made it possible to address the issue of "young/old" as one problem underlying his crisis. And not only could the latent crisis of aging be addressed here by means of the acute crisis; so could the crisis of being abandoned. Until now, he had never been left by anyone. Father and mother, both of advanced years, were still alive. He had met his wife in school; she had been his sweetheart. They had flirted with each other for a few years, then they fell in love, and they had stayed together ever since. There had been no separations. His children were married adults, but almost all of them were still living in his house, which he had expanded to accommodate them. This man was thus someone who had never experienced separation, which explains why he reacted so strongly to the "separation threat" that his wife had presented by finding a boyfriend.

Once it became possible to talk about the anxiety—his separation anxiety—behind his rage, he gained a little distance from his anger. "Now I have completely forgotten about being angry," he said suddenly.

I replied, "You should not, of course, forget that you are angry, since you really are quite angry; but sometimes it is good to get some distance from one's anger."

Then we laughed together and experienced our first moment of relaxation—a sign for me that we would be able to make contact with his crisis. For me, it is quite important to get a sense, after a certain amount of time in a crisis intervention has passed, that the person seeking help from me can relax a little just by being with me. The problem was nevertheless a long way from being resolved.

Another question to be asked in every crisis intervention is where are there resources for the affected person, sources of help, spheres of life not so seriously affected by the crisis; and of course, above all, are there relationships that can withstand the stress? In this man's case, it had already come to light that his business had basically pulled him through, and that his relationship with the pastor was able to take some stress. He had another friend with whom he often got together to talk about problems that were actually quite serious. But he felt ashamed to talk with him now about this particular problem.

He expressed it as follows: "You know, for a man like me, it is a real disaster to lose face like this."

I replied, "Yes, it must be quite hard for someone who always solves his problems by himself to suddenly have to accept help."

"Well, you know," he went on, "to lose a little face, that I can risk—but not like this; it's such a disgrace for me!"

I affirmed with my intervention that I saw him as a man who solved his own problems, representing this as a valuable quality and thus supporting his ego-complex, while simultaneously pointing out that everyone has moments of needing help.

By telling me that he could risk losing a little face, he had suggested to me that it would be possible for him to integrate something of his shadow problem. This I inferred from the hint of another problem in his statement: evidently he was not only a man who could not face getting old, and a man who panicked at the idea of being left; he was also a man not used to losing face, to having a crisis, to facing up to his own weaknesses. Thus he was a man with an enormous shadow problem, and this was surely related to his problem with aging. He was apparently someone who had to be in full possession of his powers if he was to pass in his own judgment, if he were to be judged acceptable by his ego-ideal. One is not allowed to get old or frail. One must always be one's own man. It was most likely also an expression of his shame, among other things, when he called my competence into question at the beginning of our conversation.

I formulated the problem in such a way that the issue with his wife now stood in the foreground: naturally the matter would have to discussed with her. I tried to make it clear to him that we would now experience his fear of being left by her. But we had to see how it looked from her perspective, too. Hidden behind all of this, I tried to explain, was the existential problem that he was gradually getting older, that he would have to let go of certain things, and that this was extremely difficult for him. I asked him if he had ever talked with his wife about her friendship with the other man. He looked at me in disbelief and asked me if I thought he could really talk with her. "Of course; why not?" I said. Or was it that he didn't *want* to talk with her?

Again the suspicion came to my mind that he did not have too high an opinion of women. This seemed to be another aspect of the problem which had constellated itself at the outset of our talk. Furthermore, the feeling I had had that he was taking no notice of anyone except himself seemed to be confirmed.

A crisis intervention must bring us to the point of being able to formulate a goal that is realistic and attainable within a short period of time. To be sure, this can only be achieved if we understand the fundamental issue and do not try to solve all the subsidiary issues at once. This man's problem was not difficult to grasp. He was faced, for the first time in his life, with a situation of separation. His latent aging crisis was activated, confronting him with the prospect of failure in his relationship and the loss of face that would go with it.

The following goals were established: a talk with his wife; and probably also the facilitation of a talk focused on the themes of aging, weaknesses, and the shadow, that is, parts of him that didn't fit in with his ego-ideal. It didn't seem necessary to involve other persons in the crisis intervention, nor were instrumental aids called for. By suggesting this program to him, I was giving him the message that his crisis was a wonderful opportunity to develop sides of himself that he had never needed before. He looked at me skeptically and said, "I would love to believe you, but at the moment I don't see any chance of it."

Then his misery got the better of him again. "But you will, won't you?" he burst out. "You *will* help me get my wife back! I'll give you anything you want. I'll give you my entire business. Just help me!"

This outburst once again abruptly revealed to me the depth of his crisis. It also made me wonder if he had really grasped what his crisis was all about. In response to his plea for help, I told him that it was becoming quite clear to me just how important his relationship with his wife was, but I couldn't be the one to say if she would come back to him or not. To be sure, developing a new kind of relationship with her was on the agenda, and with that I could help him. No longer warding off his anxiety by means of anger, he fell completely into its grip, collapsing into the role of a clinging child who wants to have everything again just as it was and is ready to give up everything for that. His business, as it turned out, was all he had. I tried to promise him the help that I could manage. I promised to help, but in my promise there was the suggestion that changes were needed, that it would not do simply to strive for a return to the way things had been.

At this point in our talk, I asked him about the nature of the relationship between his wife and her boyfriend. He looked at me, bewildered, and said he imagined they just went to the movies once in a while together. Then he came back to my suggestion and said it could well be that finding a new form of relationship with his wife would be important. Recently, of course, on account of his fear of her leaving him (his crisis was not so unexpected after all), he had been harassing her nonstop and had had nothing good to say about her. He thought it necessary—this was supposed to make a woman behave—but now he could see what a terrible mistake it had been. I brought him back to the situation at the beginning of the crisis intervention when he thought that I, as a woman, could not help him. Was that a comparable situation? "Yes, I think so," he replied, adding that he was much tougher with his wife than he had been with me.

I interpreted his behavior to him: his relationship with his wife really meant a lot to him, and due to anxiety about the relationship, or due to fear of losing her (she was a little older than he), he had given her a very hard time and had gotten himself into a rage. Naturally this behavior was hardly productive, although it was understandable. My intervention obviously relieved him. He let out a sigh.

I interpreted his aggressive-destructive behavior as a defense against his fear of separation. Such anxiety is experienced only when the troubled relationship is of some value. First I responded to him by interpreting his behavior, and only then did I take up his remark that such behavior could never change anything for the better.

Next I told him that he apparently had a great need to grow old together with his wife; he felt more hopeful when he imagined himself dealing with the problem of aging together with her than without her. Then, at the end of the session, he suggested that we take some more time to talk about his aging problem. And he wanted to involve his wife in our conversations after all.

His wife came along to the next few meetings. The subject really was aging, with no mention of unfaithfulness. Both confessed to having a lot of trouble with growing old. By flirting with another man, she had proved to herself that she had not yet grown too old and that she was still attractive. She had no thought of leaving her husband. The man, whom she also called her boyfriend, took her out now and then and offered her a lot of mental stimulation. He brought her interesting books to read; he gave her flowers. She felt that the quality of his attention was completely different than that of her husband, who had long since taken her presence for granted. She felt that her boyfriend took her seriously and accepted her. And this was exactly what made her husband jealous. He had sacrificed a lot in life because he thought he should always be there for his business. Now they could both see that their attitudes would have to change and, moreover, that they could.

Together they learned new behavioral strategies. They learned that one cannot simply shove conflicts away—he by working harder when conflicts arose, she by walking all over him—but that conflicts must really be talked about! It was a wonderful experience to see them both learn an alternative to telling each other that he or she is good for nothing; one could also say, "It makes me feel bad when you. . . ."

The other matter was learning to deal with their own shadow aspects, learning to face the realities of not being perfect, of not being able to stay forever at the peak of their lives, of getting weaker and less attractive, or rather of having to learn how to be attractive in new ways.

These were the essential behavioral strategies that they learned. We also spoke about the possibility of the husband's parents dying—as a preventive crisis intervention, so to speak, and yet not unrelated to the theme of the crisis itself. And then with great caution the possibility was broached of their own deaths. It was remarkable how very hard they both tried to imagine themselves in these situations, but it only went so far as imagining their parents dying, and that with the qualifying certainty that their parents wouldn't die for a long, long time.

I believe the actual crisis intervention took place in the first and second hours.

The prerequisite of this crisis intervention was the man's willingness to open himself up to the pastor. The pastor, frightened by his boundless rage, sought further help. The pastor's fright accurately reflected the theme of the crisis: panic. My first response was simply to listen to the man's outbursts of rage. Then I encouraged him to imagine what a new life situation would mean for him. This allowed him to get a sense of the anxiety dominating him, and we were able to discover the background problems in his life that urgently needed resolution, problems which could transform him and give his relationship new energy. In keeping with his inclination to take the bull by the horns—and probably in keeping with my own nature—I was a bit hasty in pointing out the creative possibilities inherent in his situation. This made his fear flare up again quite noticeably. Another explanation of his response is that he could only admit to being in the power of his fear when he could see a way out of it. Basically, I tried to choose interventions and interpretations that would confirm his self-esteem. Thus I proceeded in a manner which was in the broadest sense "defense-oriented," that is, I followed the lead of his defenses in order to strengthen his ego-complex first, reserving my treatment of the issues coming up for a second step.

We worked together for another six hours, following up on the actual crisis intervention.

Three years later this couple came for another crisis intervention when the man's father and mother died, one right after the other. It seems important to mention this here, since one often gets the impression that a crisis intervention, in the shortest possible time, can solve a problem that long-term therapy can not. This is not the case. Crisis interventions have their place when someone is stuck in a crisis and when, depending on the crisis, new behavioral possibilities can be discovered in a great leap forward. The issues get addressed, and afterward many persons continue working on the same problems without going into therapy. But it definitely happens—and not seldom—that after a crisis intervention a person is glad to be emotionally his or her "old self" again, without having tackled the underlying problems. Here an image comes to mind from Balint, who says that a crisis intervention can be likened to the process of freeing up a tree trunk that has been snagged as it was floating down a river. The tree trunk continues its course down the river on its own. Crisis interventions that proceed in this way are certainly the nicest. But very often, the rivers on which we float are already quite overgrown, and the tree trunks keep getting themselves wedged in again.

Chapter 3

Dealing with Emotion and Inhibition

In this category two kinds of crisis can be distinguished from each other, according to their strikingly different outward appearances.

Overstimulated individuals are carried away by their emotions: fear, rage, love, and other forms of arousal. They get flooded; ego-consciousness is not able to hold the emotion within bounds. Such crises impress us with their "loudness" which makes them recognizable by nearly everyone. Individuals in this condition need to be calmed down and to regain their composure. In other words, they must find their way back to their habitual defense mechanisms without, however, repressing the new element: a constellated complex that is expressing itself in the flood of emotion. It is usually quite simple to discern the situation precipitating these crises. Problems lurking in the background are more difficult to track down.

Then there are "silent" crises, which often pass unseen. In these crises, individuals are completely paralyzed by their own control. Cutting off their emotions from conscious life, they seem to have everything shipshape. And yet their lives grow steadily emptier, especially when situations of separation and loss are added to the picture. At the peak of their crises, nothing is any good any more—there is no point in anything, nor do they find this any reason for alarm. All the stimulation normally radiating from life seems to be lacking.

If overstimulated persons are completely carried away and controlled by emotion, understimulated persons are dominated by the control of emotion.

Both forms of crisis—compared with the crisis in the creative process—can be seen as expressions of the phase of incubation. In one case, raw unconscious processes flood consciousness. In the other, huge sums of energy are mobilized in order to prevent processes that are taking place in the unconscious from influencing the conscious attitude.

A Crisis of Overstimulation

A woman requested a crisis intervention. She said she was at the end of her rope. She came looking disheveled, and it was obvious that she had hardly slept. Very tense and fidgety, she started right in: "I am in a mess, and I need someone to help me get my feet back on the ground. I think it is right for me to be going through this, even if it hurts a lot. But I don't know if I'm coming or going. I don't even know if I can speak so that you'll understand. I've fallen in love with a man. It has never been so intense in all my life. I'm thirty-nine and have been married for fifteen years. I had no idea there even was such a thing—this storm of feelings, this openness, this passion. I am really aglow, flaming with desire. I talk like a teenager. But that's just the way it is. I'm mad with longing, inspired, and it's burning me up. The crazy part of it is, this man doesn't want my love, doesn't reciprocate. But that doesn't kill my love; it only makes it more desperate and full of longing. Something inside of me has gotten loose. I don't know what I should do about it. I don't know how I should live with it. Sometimes I think I'll take this man by storm. But he has said to me, clear as a bell, that he may have friendly feelings for me, but he is afraid of the intensity of my feelings, and doesn't himself feel anything like what I feel."

She started to cry. "It's enough to drive you crazy. It takes almost forty years for love to break out, and at whom? Someone who doesn't want me. It's all I can think about, this love. My husband—I don't know what I'm going to do about him. My children think I'm off my rocker. I forget everything. I can barely keep my most important appointments. [She is self-employed and works part-time.] I'm starting to get more and more afraid about what's going to happen to my nicely ordered life. That I could land in such a mess—I never would have thought it possible."

After this outpouring she looked at me expectantly. I felt flooded, but at the same time alive and concerned. In my mind's eye I saw another huge wave of emotions on the horizon, and I asked myself what had been set in motion. In case of emergency, I reminded myself, I could always send her to a physician for tranquilization. And so I decided to embark on a crisis intervention. I felt concerned about the crisis, but at the same time, in the back of my mind, I questioned whether her overstimulated condition could be sufficiently moderated by talking and relating to me. Since she was flooded by emotions, the point would be to control them in such a way that their animating effect could be preserved without threatening her ego-complex.

"It can make us anxious," I told her, "when we have been living a very ordered life and then such a storm of emotions descends on us."

She beamed at me briefly, "Yes, but I *feel* myself as never before. Everything about me—and everything in my life—could go to pieces. That scares me." While I was addressing her anxiety, confirming her obvious ability under normal circumstances to keep her conflicts and emotions under control (otherwise she wouldn't have had a well-ordered life until now), she was expressing her joy over these previously unknown emotions. This was a sign that she basically had a well-structured ego capable of finding a place in her life for these new, if at present chaotic, emotions. She was also able to describe her crisis quite vividly. She experienced it as a flooding by something completely new. These new feelings were something of great importance to her; that much she knew. What she didn't know was whether she was coming or going. Anxieties that had not yet shown their true colors were hidden within. It was already evident that she did not want to live without these new emotions, even though they would be bringing big problems along with them.

Next she talked at greater length about her joy in these new feelings, their liveliness, and yet how fear arose whenever she wanted to give her herself over to her joy. One notices a great number of repetitions in the transcript of our talk. Seized by powerful emotions, we often repeat ourselves. Such repetitions can be viewed as a structure that gradually contains emotion and prevents it from flooding. A later segment of our talk ran as follows:

She: Yes, I always thought I was a very controlled woman.
I: It is especially hard when one relies on control and then suddenly such a storm of feelings breaks out.
She: But also especially nice. Secretly I always thought something in life was missing. It's such a double bind: I want the passion, but it could cost me dearly.
I: What are you thinking of?
She: If I choose the wrong men to pursue, that undermines my self-esteem. If I meet someone who reciprocates my feelings, then my family is in danger.
I: You are afraid of being humiliated, and you are afraid for your marriage. You are afraid of losing these passionate feelings again, and you are afraid of letting them into your life.
She: You know, it's so painful—when someone can awaken such love in a woman and then not want to have her. It's humiliating, unthinkably humiliating. Of course, I told myself that he's just a coward, a hen-pecked husband, someone who is afraid of feelings. But then again, I think he's too wonderful to be put down like that. So I put myself down. I must have some kind of misprogrammed instinct: his not wanting me only makes my love stronger.

We worked together on a social project—that's where we got to know and care for each other. We are both very committed people. A week ago he told me that he was so committed because as a boy he suffered from the same problems which we are trying to alleviate in our project. That set off the spark. But I had already dreamt of him. And then when I told him of my love, he sort of stiffened all up inside. He had no desire whatsoever to hurt me, but he rejected me unmistakably.
I: He awakened your feelings, your passionate side, but didn't want it all aimed at him.
She: Maybe it's enough that he awakened them.
I: Could you look at it that way?
She: I don't like to, but I can—I probably have to.

Here she introduced a creative notion. She got away from the notion that she must either have this man or be humiliated. She took up the idea that it might be enough for him to have awakened her feelings. The talk had relieved her of some anxiety, and her creativity was able to emerge as soon as her anxiety had been reduced. Anxiety blocks the creative process.

She continued, "The thought keeps occurring to me that I don't feel this way about my husband, that he never awakened these kinds of feelings in me. We have a good relationship. He is very reliable, level-headed, and loving with me and the children. But there is no ecstasy, no exuberance of feeling. Actually, he has always been more like a father to me, and I have always liked it that way. Strange I never thought of that before, but it's true. A relationship with the man I have fallen in love with would require so much more of me. He would expect more initiative and stimulation from me, more sharing of responsibility. I can also see things with him getting out of order, maybe even chaotic. But when I think of his fear of my feelings, it makes me wonder if I'm not just dreaming the whole thing up."

I suggested that the importance of this "love-storm" might be her experience of herself as more tender and loving, rather than more passionately ardent than ever before, but also that the storm showed how important it was for her to change her relationship with her husband along the lines of her fantasies about the man who had awakened her feelings. Thus I interpreted the crisis to her as a potential enrichment of her life, as a stimulus to growth latent in the marital relationship. I addressed the developmental theme behind the precipitating event.

In response, she asked herself whether the crisis might not rather be a sign that she and her husband had been fooling themselves for half of their lives. This was possible, I conceded, and went on to explain that in the course of a lifetime, one's longings for what can and should be lived in a relationship constantly change. These changes are also crises of maturation. Only seldom do such longings break out in both partners at the same time. When this happens, the relationship must either undergo a transfor-mation or else fall apart completely.[1] I viewed her falling in love and her outbreak of stormy emotions as signs that she had become strong enough psychically in the course of her life to withstand this emotional upheaval and the complications attending it. But I could also understand if she preferred to put aside her marital problem and avoid the crisis.

I was attempting to interpret her problem to her, to point out developmental possibilities, and to address strengths she possessed in abundance. But I was also giving her the option of an escape route that would afford her temporary sanctuary from her marital crisis, as well as indirect avoidance of a justified fear.

"But then I'm not giving us any chance at all," she objected. "Why shouldn't my husband be able to change, too? Maybe he also has other longings—still!"

Allowing her to cope with the crisis by means of defense—or escape—made it possible for her to consider the significance of the crisis looming up in her marriage, to tolerate thoughts about it, and even to hope for a change in the relationship.

"I believe I can sleep again," she concluded. "I'm not going to take the man of my dreams by storm, no matter how hard this is to accept. I can deal with the humiliation. I'm going to start paying attention to the world of feelings; maybe I'll even write things down. My marriage is going into a crisis. I'll try to convey my longings to my husband and stop misusing him as a father. My feelings are just as chaotic as before but now I have the right perspective. I believe this crisis will change my life." We made an appointment to talk again in three days.

The crisis intervention was able to direct this woman's attention to a perspective on crisis as transformation, to strengthen her feeling that something important was happening with her, but also to show that her fear was justified. The point was that

she would have to accept new facets of herself completely. This could not be easy for
a woman very used to being in control. In addition, she had to suffer the rejection of
her love and the revelation of problems in her marriage.

The phase of insight had already been reached. These new emotions threw light on
her relationship with her husband, revealing the need for change. The storm of
feelings coursing through her would force her to reconstruct her self-image as well.

She arrived three days later looking calmer and more rested, and reported that she
was getting along better now. She no longer saw being in love simply as an adolescent
crisis; it was a great enrichment. But her marriage crisis was already under way. She
had talked with her husband about her new feelings and longings, but she hadn't
been able to make herself understood. He had insisted that she had always had a good
life. He did not see why he should change a good thing. She had reached the point of
considering separation when she had a dream which she thought might have something important to say.

Persons undergoing crises often dream. Accurately illuminating the crisis from the
perspective of the unconscious, these dreams often herald the emergence of creative
transformations. In my experience, dreams in crisis situations are relatively easy to
understand. The simplicity and clarity of such dreams can be explained in conjunction
with the mental state that a crisis situation evokes: defense mechanisms are less
strongly organized than usual, the ego-complex is less coherent, and the energy of the
life dynamic flows in one direction only, namely, toward the crisis. The dream:

> I have given birth to a child, and I am puzzled because I don't remember
> having been pregnant. It is a very sweet little girl. I smother her with hugs
> and kisses, the way newborns can take it. My husband comes into the room.
> I am embarrassed because I don't know if he is the father. He says we will
> see if he could be the father. I am relieved. But he doesn't look at the child;
> he goes to work at his computer.

What stood out most in regard to feelings, the dreamer reported, was joy in the
newborn child. She understood her dream as telling her that her crisis had brought
something really new into being (birth), but that the difficulties could not be ignored.
At the moment her husband was more interested in the computer than in the child.
I pointed out to her that he reacted to the child in a relatively friendly fashion,
considering he did not recognize it as his own. That would be a generous way of
handling the situation, not to mention his remark that they would see if he could be
the father. He must have been asking for time and was probably dealing with the crisis
initially by burying himself in his hobby. She replied that she would have liked a
quicker solution. From the dream I inferred that a solution was not yet within reach.

Although this crisis plunged the woman into great hardship, changed her sense of
identity, and brought forth fantasies of relationship that were difficult to live out with
her partner of many years, it nevertheless gave birth to an entirely new emotional
realm of experience. New impulses, already present for some time, succeeded in
drawing every aspect of this woman's life into the crisis. Her capacity to receive these

new impulses delivered her marital relationship into its own transformative crisis. The crisis itself is not the creative thing. Here it was the availability of creative impulses, of transformative aspects, and of new behavioral options that immersed a human existence in crisis. The sudden and dramatic quality of the crisis was no doubt attributable to the tenacity of her defenses against these impulses. The crisis stepped in when newness no longer allowed itself to be shut out, when transformation took the matter out of her hands, filling her with pain. This is another meaning of crisis intervention: the capacity to take in the new, to accept the way life changes, to make room for novelty in life as it is lived, and to be prepared for the psychological and social risks involved.

Even if life changes creatively, it does not necessarily become easier to live. It does, however, become livelier.

It was crucial for this woman to share an experience with a human being who could receive it without judging. Then she, too, could welcome change. She could find a place for the erotic complex, which no longer pestered her in an overstimulated way, but was invited into her life in all its richness.

A Crisis of Understimulation

A sixty-nine-year-old man was referred to me for a consultation, possibly a crisis intervention. He had suddenly become strange, his physician reported to me. The physician had known the man for some time, but during this appointment he had sensed something alien and had had difficulty establishing any rapport with him. The patient, who suffered from various functional disorders, always roughly the same ones, was referred to me in an authoritarian fashion, on account of the physician's anxiety and uneasiness.

A plainly dressed, rather short man looking composed, gray, and reserved came to see me. As he sat down, I had the feeling of being totally superfluous. And yet he was obviously waiting for me to say something. As impatience mounted within me, I asked myself what in the world he could want. Why had the physician insisted that I see him so promptly? Was he really in a crisis? I took note of this remarkable feeling of being unnecessary. I asked him for some dates from his biography. He gave them to me, curtly. He had played a leading role in a business that he had been instrumental in building together with a colleague. At sixty-three he had relinquished his position to his son. In all, he had two sons and a daughter. One of the sons and the daughter lived in America. His wife had died two years ago. He closed his brief recital with the sentence, "But the physician could have told you all of that."

I replied that I would have asked him again anyway, in order to get a sense of what it all meant to him emotionally.

He: [dryly] I'm through with that.
I: It must have been difficult to bear this series of losses.

He: You see, I survived.
I: Well yes, that is certainly important.

I asked him more about his physical complaints.

He: That is the physician's concern.
I: Yes, you're right, but I have to know about it, too, to get the whole picture.
He: No one can do that anyway; that's why Doctor X sent me to you.
I: You're very disappointed that no one can get a picture of your situation.
He: Disappointed? Outraged! But what does it matter? I suppose you have a theory?
[He threw this out as if to say, "Why don't we just quit wasting our time?"]
I: Do you have one?
He: Now you want me to do your work, too.
I: I sense that you are very lonely. I feel as if I am totally unnecessary, except to give you a target for your anger. I have the impression that I could never satisfy you, and I conclude from this that you feel totally unnecessary on the face of the earth . . . and that you are angry about that.

Understanding my sense of superfluousness as a countertransference phenomenon—as a feeling or fantasy precipitated in me out of my empathic relatedness to another person—I returned the feeling to him as his. He had been projecting it onto his various discussion partners, who, as a result of the projection, were in fact rendered unnecessary and unable to do anything right for him. Projection had provided him with a way to deny his own sense of worthlessness.

While offering him this interpretation, I was thinking of Ringel's presuicidal syndrome.[2] I had the impression that this man's life, becoming increasingly bound by limitations, was in the process of closing in on itself. At this point his aggression would still be experienced as directed at others; it would turn inward if the narrowing tendency continued. However, I did not want to address the issue of suicidal fantasies yet. His first response to my interpretation was, "You think it is difficult to get over so many losses?"

Here he accepted the confirmation of his self-worth which I had offered in our talk some time before. He veered away from his feelings of abandonment and superfluousness, but began to take me seriously. I breathed a sigh of relief, for I had the sense that I had found a place within his narrowed world from which I could begin to open things up.

I assured him that I found it practically impossible for anyone to work through so many losses in such a short time. The first hint of a relaxed smile flickered across his face. But he did not continue, so I said, "Most people in a comparable situation of loss rescue themselves by means of bravery. Feelings are not allowed to exist at all, since the first feeling to come up would be grief. Instead the stomach aches or ties itself in a knot. Life is no longer to be enjoyed, and the future fades away."

He listened and nodded. This made me stop talking. "Don't let me interrupt your lecture," he said, looking directly at me.

"It can make one angry at others, thinking about how healthy they still are," I replied. I interpreted his anger to him as an understandable reaction.

He raised his eyebrows confirmingly. "Yes, I am angry, and I am also very lonely—lonely and proud."

"And you sometimes think you could put an end to it all?"

Startled, he looked at me and nodded. Then his face closed up again, "But what are we talking about? There's no point in it!"

I: It's unnerving suddenly to talk about such secret ruminations. And you aren't allowed to accept any help.

He: You walk all over me the whole time with your tricks. What if I do go ahead and kill myself?

I: I can't stop you. In the final analysis that is your decision. But there is no return. So you have to be pretty sure that the experiment of life has nothing more to offer.

He: [bitterly] The experiment of life indeed! You can talk. You still have time. You have work. You are respected. You can keep in touch with others. I have to live without all of that. And in the meantime I'm getting older every day.

The extent of his problem was now plain to see. Loss of work had made him feel superfluous, robbed him of his self-esteem, and taken away his sense of being respected. Consequently, he judged himself no longer capable of maintaining contact with others. Behind the problem of contact, though, other issues appeared to be lurking. And there was the very real pressure of time running out in his life.

We are dealing here with a form of crisis totally different from the one in the first example. If that woman seemed overstimulated, a state that could be pictured as a river at high water, then this man was understimulated, like a dried-out riverbed which had seen no water for some time. And yet, hardly had he sat down when the central issue was already constellated between us. I interpreted my feeling of superfluousness as his feeling, which he kept guarded behind a defensive posture. By relating to him on the basis of such feelings, I was able to bridge the gap between us; and then he was able to begin opening up to me. Here is another example of someone who had reached a point in life where things could no longer go on as they had. Something had to change if death was not to seem like an attractive alternative. The physician had seen this quite plainly when his relationship with the man was disrupted by the crisis. There was no event that might have caused the crisis to come to a head, at least none we could identify. I find it more likely that a narrowing trend had been developing in degrees too small to be noticeable, until it suddenly erupted as a crisis. This development might have been critical for some time, but not until now did it emerge as a crisis proper. Such a crisis is less impressive for its abundance than for its virtual lack of emotion. And yet in every case there comes an unavoidable moment when the crisis presses for a decision. Since for me the central theme of this man's crisis was superfluousness, I felt that he should recall a life situation in which he had still been able to accomplish something. I had noticed that he welcomed interpretations preserving his self-esteem, which is not surprising given the centrality of the theme of superfluousness.

So I asked him, "As long as you were still working you felt respected, so you didn't feel superfluous then, did you?"

"No, just imagine: I had an enormous responsibility. . . ." Then followed a detailed account of his professional life. Professional pride radiated forth, with no trace of being unnecessary—quite the contrary.

"At least no one can take away these experiences," I commented.

He looked at me, taken aback. "Yes, I suppose one could see it that way, too," he said. "But things are different now. I have handed the whole business over to my son. He is in the prime of his youth, and the business has become more than I can deal with. I have had to put aside so much in my life. Actually I wanted to go to the opera, and I have made a resolution for the later years of my life to hear as much opera as possible. But now I don't want to anymore; I don't care to go alone. My son—I was hoping he would need my advice. But he manages just fine. I'm really *not* necessary. We could talk about a project once in a while. He could still do whatever he wants. But such an exchange would be important for me."

I: Have you said that to him?

He: [indignantly] No. He has to find that out for himself!

I: Let me make a comparison. You can decide if it works. At the beginning of our talk, I had the feeling that I was perfectly unnecessary. We have understood this feeling of superfluousness, which presented itself to me, as a reflection of your *feeling* unnecessary in your present life-situation. But it could be that, *fearing* you are unnecessary, you convey to everyone you meet the feeling that neither their conversation nor their company makes any difference. Your conversation partners naturally withdraw, and you are left with the feeling of not being needed.

Thus I interpreted the initial constellation which had taken shape at the beginning of our counseling as a problem of relationship.

After thinking it over for a while he said, quite affected, "I guess I do it with everyone, not just with my son. But with him in particular. I did it with my wife, too. And I never realized it."

While the feeling of being unnecessary must have crystallized when he gave up his work, I had the impression of a much deeper life problem hiding in the background. I asked him if he had ever felt unnecessary while still working.

He: Not at work, but otherwise yes. You see, I was an absolutely unnecessary child, the eleventh of a poor weaver, born during the First World War. I was superfluous. And when I noticed that, I decided to become something. That I accomplished, which is why resigning was so hard.

I: I find it astonishing that you were able to hand the business over when it held such importance for you.

He: Well, you know, my son is very competent, and then there will soon be grandchildren. But yes, you're right; it was very hard. One day I was a company man and the next day a private man.

I: How did you feel at the time—can you still remember?

He: Oh yes—completely worthless, without any ideas. I was apathetic, I had no interests and no energy for anything. And yet I actually would have had time. So I was very disappointed in myself.

I: That is a trap that many people fall into when they retire. They lose so much. They lose the sense of significance that the business has accustomed them to. They lose their feeling of effectiveness, of being important to others, sometimes of being anyone at all. A new phase of life begins. Now they have to rearrange everything inside, make room for all the feelings of disappointment and emptiness, detach themselves, remind themselves of what can't be taken away, contemplate the new life phase, the new freedom. This doesn't happen overnight; it's a time of major reorientation.

He: You mean it happens this way to others, too? This is a known condition?

I: One speaks of retirement depression.

He: I was always so brave. Even when it hurt, I always gritted my teeth. And then, before I knew it, my wife got sick, was sick already. It was not a nice time—and then she died. I moved out of the house into an apartment, away from the old neighbors who had known me.

This man had experienced a series of separation situations piled on top of each other, some of which he had brought on himself, without considering the fact that separations are difficult to bear. Not only had he fallen into loneliness; he had helped himself to it. He had buried the entire extent of his grief, replacing it with a hard and bitter exterior, which also shielded him from himself. As the hour drew to a close he said, "The physician referred me for an hour's consultation. Can I come another few times? I have to straighten this out, especially the matter of being unnecessary and the problem with feelings."

I asked him how he felt now—a superfluous question, judging from the new life in his face. The crisis intervention had brought him into connection with me. No longer would he have to solve his problems all by himself. The intervention had made him aware of his problems of isolation and grief and their relation to his functional disorders. The value of this was not merely diagnostic. He had established his own contact with these problems and had turned his attention to his crisis, especially in regard to the feeling of superfluousness. Equipped with a new perspective, he was now able to take swift measures against this feeling and against his habit of declaring others to be unnecessary. He hadn't been a "doer" his entire life for nothing. Discussing the matter with his son and with former friends, he was informed that he now saw correctly how it had been. But now that he had this contact, things were different. Reaching out to others, he was both stimulating and stimulated.

Suddenly he was outraged to discover that he could not help thinking about his dead wife. I informed him that, for all his bravery, he had sidestepped grief and in the process sacrificed those feelings that connected him to her. He could now mourn her

loss belatedly; I would guide him along. The mourning process, a process of transformation, occurs in phases comparable to those of the creative process. To grieve
creatively means to discover what life shared with the other has opened up in us, to
reconsider and relive it consciously, to bring to awareness especially those sides of
ours which this special person was the first to awaken and love into existence, to try
them out as one's own possibilities in life. The loss not only depletes us—it does this,
too—but also enriches us, if it is worked through. In this time of memories, conflicts
are bound to resurface, too. Behavioral peculiarites in the relationship will be scruti-
nized. For example, this man came to the conclusion that it was actually his wife who
had been interested in opera, not himself, which explained why he sometimes wanted
to go to the opera and yet did not go. I asked him if her interest might not have
awakened his interest; it would be strange if his interest had died along with his wife.
In fact, his interest had not died. Before long, he was organizing trips to the opera in
Milan, and on the way the elders of the group wittily debated the question of whether
they were, in Brecht's formulation, "unworthy" old folk.

Out of this work of mourning, new possibilities emerged, which he tested out right
away in his interactions with others. The crisis intervention grew into an on-going
therapeutic relationship. He developed an interest in his dreams and always found a
reason to continue meeting once every three weeks. (He is now seventy-six years old.)

The narrow ledge of this man's life was both the origin of his crisis and the point
where it had left him standing. There seemed to be no exit from the precipice except
into the void. If it had not been for the physician's intervention, he probably would
have let himself die. The crisis intervention returned to him the rich realm of his
feeling-life, freeing his energy. But it also initiated a very unpleasant confrontation
with aggressive, power-hungry traits of whose existence he had been quite unaware.
The crisis brought to birth what his life had lacked and what he had regarded until then
as a disturbance to be avoided: not only aggression, but the entire spectrum of emotions.
One can clearly see with this man how crisis marks the passageway to transformation,
where success and failure represent equally possible outcomes. I believe that this same
case could just as easily have ended in failure.

As with crises of overstimulation, so with crises whose most noticeable quality is a
lack of stimulation, the main problem is caused by the activity of a repressed element.
Held under control and excluded from life, the repressed element pushes forward
with increasing vigor. In response, control tightens its grip. The result is an enormous
constriction of life. If those persons who are caught in a crisis of understimulation
seek out contact with a helping person, they can then integrate into their lives the
themes pressing for recognition. However, opening up is for such persons a difficult
matter; it makes life less predictable and generates more anxiety.

Individuals with this form of control and defensive social manner are not likely to
seek help. As in the case of the man described here, they often provoke crises in their
environment or with other persons. Only then do their fellows become aware of that
strangely stagnant form of crisis that manifests itself above all in a narrowness become
intolerable.

Chapter 4

The Threat of Suicide

When the topic of crisis intervention arises, many people immediately think of suicide prevention. Suicide commonly serves as an expression for existential crisis in general; yet it can also be understood as a way of coping with crisis. Threatened by a totally devastating situation, exposed to naked terror, suicidal persons attempt to kill themselves in order to forestall the anticipated catastrophe. The example of suicide shows us many of the components of a crisis, especially the narrowing of life possibilities, the constriction of emotions, the inability to carry out a decision aggressively, and the incapacity to solve problems creatively. If an outer problem is added to the situation, most often a direct insult or an unfulfillable demand (which is also a wound to self-esteem), then suicide can be experienced as the only remaining way out. I often get the impression that for someone with suicidal tendencies, the mere fact of a crisis occurring at all is mortifying. Suicide quite clearly demonstrates how an individual can emerge either transformed from a crisis, with new life possibilities, or else with no more life possibilities at all.

Among the survivors of suicide attempts, we find some who have undergone very deep changes as a result of their experience. Hillman describes the killing of oneself as perhaps the greatest of all psychic transformations and says that there are persons who commit suicide in order to transform themselves radically.[1] This is corroborated by a statement we sometimes hear to the effect that survivors of suicide attempts have the feeling of having been granted life anew. They want life. They feel, perhaps for the first time in their lives, something like a justification for existence. They sense that they were not created merely to die. They suddenly come into attunement with life and solve their problems without difficulty. These individuals are happy that someone brought them back again. They sometimes recount transcendental experiences similar to those reported by persons who were clinically dead and subsequently resuscitated. Central is their experience of having attempted to throw life away, in spite of which they are still alive today. Taking this as a judgment of God, they are conscious of a whole new set of possibilities in life suddenly opening up to them. They were, after all, allowed to live.

There is another reaction to an unsuccessful suicide attempt: little changed by the experience, some persons remain in need of treatment. They may be happy that they were rescued, or they may not be. They complain that the suicide attempt didn't

change anything, that all their problems are still there. Shortly after regaining consciousness, most suicidal persons can be readily addressed in regard to their problems.
Their defenses are still quite weakened. Later they are considerably more difficult to
reach and are quick to deny their problems again. Hence the importance of carrying
out a crisis intervention during the coming-to period.

Then there is one last, very large group: persons whom the suicide attempt leaves
with serious physical injuries. That a suicide attempt can lead to permanent physical
damage, which in the case of survival must be lived with, is something seldom
considered by those attempting suicide.

In general, crisis interventions with suicidal persons are, if possible, to be carried
out before any attempts are made, and at the latest, immediately after the victim
returns to consciousness. Lucid theories are available for crisis interventions with
suicidal crises, as are guidelines on how they should be conducted. These guidelines
are considerably less ambiguous than for other crises. Public mental-health and church-
related counseling institutions attach great importance to crisis-intervention centers.
Outer instrumental aids are widely diversified and well known. Whenever instrumental aids are widely diversified, we are dealing with a problem whose importance and
intricacy has long been recognized and about which, therapeutically, perplexity and
pessimism prevail.

In Switzerland in 1985 there were some 1,600 deaths from suicide, more deaths
than those caused by traffic accidents. It is estimated that for every successful suicide,
ten to twenty suicide attempts are made. The estimated number of unreported cases
is extraordinarily high. According to age, the highest concentrations occur between
fifteen and thirty, and between fifty-five and sixty-five.[2]

The causes of suicide are problems of self-esteem in the broadest sense, loneliness,
lack of contact, aggression, and social deprivation. Risk groups have been ranked in
the following order:

— persons who are dependent on drugs,
— depressed persons,
— isolated persons,
— persons who have already made an attempt, and
— members of the helping professions.[3]

Suicide as an act of impulse is differentiated from suicide as an act of premeditation.
Premeditated acts of suicide are often encountered among the elderly. Secretly weighing what life could still want from them against what life could still offer to them, they
reach the conclusion that the effort they must make no longer tallies with whatever
reward they might get out of it, in which case they no longer wish to live. A famous
representative of premeditated suicide is Jean Amery. Having written a book on death
by choice (Freitod), in which he confronted himself with the prospect of suicide, he
committed suicide on his sixtieth birthday.[4] This is a virtual classic of premeditated
suicide: first a book is written in which taking one's life is posited as a legitimate

alternative to putting up with life; then the book is followed with the act itself. There is little of the act of impulse here. But one can never—even here—be totally sure.

The following is an example of a premeditated suicide. An eighty-four-year-old woman made an attempt on her life. She was discovered and admitted to a hospital. When she came to, she was furious with everyone in whose care she had been. Having assumed that it was her right at eighty-four to decide whether she wanted to live or not, she felt that she was quite capable of taking responsibility for her own actions. She was alone in the world, sick, had no more money, her last friend had died, and the week before her dog had died, too. She affirmed that she would do it again, which only succeeded in having her transferred to a psychiatric hospital. Such situations pose considerable difficulties for caretakers. Can we accept an individual's intention to kill him or herself? Must we save life at any cost?

That an attempt at suicide is most often an act of impulse becomes apparent when one considers the fact that four out of five suicidal persons are no longer suicidal after coming to; by then, the acute crisis is over. Hence the obvious importance of crisis intervention in advance of the attempt. Crisis intervention with suicidal persons is, however, enormously difficult. Toward every sort of crisis we each have personal attitudes that are colored by our individual life histories, value systems, and problems. The position we take toward suicide seems especially complicated to me.

There are therapists whose aim is to dissuade suicidal persons from their intentions at any cost. Other therapists believe that a suicidal intention should be understood as a symptom or a symbol, and its inner meaning reflected on in order to work through the psychic situation: the suicidal impulse is to be "seen through." A classic representative of the latter thesis is Hillman, who advises that therapists accompany patients in their longing for death.[5] It is my opinion that if we are not only to talk theoretically about suicide, but also to deal with it in practice, a great deal of detachment is required to recommend unhesitatingly that patients be accompanied in their longing for death. Most therapists keep in mind both perspectives outlined above. Naturally we do not want a patient to commit suicide. That would be dreadful. But then again we do not want to maintain the unqualified expectation that it is possible to live without any suicidal thoughts or impulses. Such an expectation would be totally unrealistic, lacking the slightest understanding of someone with suicidal tendencies. A suicidal impulse is a very important impulse, and also a very important symbol. It is quite extraordinary when someone seizes on a means no less radical than death in order to break off a dynamic before it has reached its peak, basically allowing the crisis no chance. If a suicidal person becomes aware that a therapist has left the choice open between continuing to live and dying, that person will most likely choose life.

This is an exceedingly difficult situation for therapists, who are constantly confronted with the question of hospitalization. The suicidal state is hardly a state in which to make a genuine choice between life and death. Wouldn't it be wiser, therefore, to protect such individuals from themselves? Or, on the contrary, might someone in a suicidal state experience commitment to a hospital as the final, decisive wound, and as the first really convincing confirmation of his or her wish to die? The risk of acting

falsely is unusually high. And since life itself is at stake—one of our highest values—
the situation is saturated with anxiety, which we may defend ourselves against by
means of rage. In the final analysis, we therapists cannot decide whether or not an
individual will take his or her life. If we think we can pass judgment on the life and
death of another human being, then we have identified with that fantasy of omnipotence so easily delegated to us by the suicidal person. Every book on suicide repeatedly
emphasizes that no one is lord over life and death. The fact that this point is so often
emphasized indicates that we must fight the strong temptation to assume such a role.
It is relieving for most suicidal persons to be approached with the notion that suicide
is a serious motif in life, a symbol whose meaning must be discovered, as in the case
of every other symbol. For the meaning of suicide is not limited to killing one's self.
Suicide should be seen from a much broader perspective: surely it has to do with the
temptation to run away before something actually comes to a climax. Suicide can thus
be seen as a symbol for a premature attempt at transformation. But we also need to
ask what must be added to the as-yet incomplete transformation in order for it to be
brought to real fruition.

The most important factor influencing our encounter with suicide is our attitude
toward it. So we must begin by assessing and then accepting our own suicidal potential.
We must ask ourselves how much we fear our own suicidal tendencies. Each of us
has a suicidal side. We all know the suicidal impulse to one degree or another. Often
thought of as a last resort, it can give us a way to cope with crisis, that is, an emergency
exit. If we therapists are too successful in repressing our own suicidal themes, we will
end up fighting them in our projections onto suicidal persons, who can then use their
potential for suicide as a powerful weapon to manipulate us. In such cases the suicide
is no longer the patient's private affair, and a successful attempt would call into
question the therapist's identity as well. We should not overlook the fact that there is
no better way to manipulate than with a suicidal threat or attempt. Thus an integral
part of the crisis intervention consists of discovering at whom the suicide is directed.
However, it is also quite wrong in my opinion to see only manipulation and revenge,
without sensing the great anxiety, helplessness, and powerlessness behind suicide.

To be able to deal with suicidal crises, however, more is required than identifying
and taking responsibility for our own suicidal potential. We must also reflect on the
problem of death in general, as well as on the potential meaninglessness of life itself.
And we must view all this in the context of what it means to fail. I agree with the
opinion of many psychotherapists that failure is a crucial dimension of suicidal potential, for failing is precisely the thing that persons with suicidal tendencies cannot
accept. Perhaps they have something in common here with members of the helping
professions. That we so readily link failing with suicide could suggest that we do
indeed have fantasies of omnipotence in relation to suicidal persons, fantasies that
prevent us from being able to allow something to fail, to let someone die if need be.
On the one hand, suicidal persons almost court our omnipotence. After all, nothing
less than life is at stake. Pleading, often very urgently, for help, they are giving
expression to this sense that everything hangs in the balance. On the other hand, they

can very easily disparage us by saying, for example, that the good-for-nothing therapist wants only to cash in on their misery. Or, directing a "mere" tirade of hate at a colleague, they displace the aggressive attack.

Thus they provoke the very rejection of which they are so afraid, and at the same time they put their therapists to the test. Frequently they transfer their bad interpersonal experiences onto the therapist, and if the hate is not felt directly, it is often experienced in the countertransference: the therapist feels hate because he or she should help but may not, hate as a mirroring of the hate in the suicidal person, hate as a reaction to being seduced into feeling omnipotent and worthless at the same time, rage as a reaction to the great uncertainty and anxiety. These problems can be handled much more adequately if the therapist anticipates an expression of hate, an expectation of grandiose help, and a disparagement of his or her own person. Therapists can cope more effectively if they understand these reactions as transferences of bad interpersonal experiences, and thus can avoid taking the hate personally.

Also affecting our attitudes toward suicidal persons in the crisis intervention are the various views of suicide held by the psychotherapeutic schools and orientations we represent.

In this regard I would like to cite two passages from Jung in which he takes a position on suicide. Both dated July 1946, they are from letters written, oddly enough, almost consecutively. From the first letter:

> The idea of suicide, understandable as it is, does not seem commendable to me. We live in order to attain the greatest possible amount of spiritual development and self-awareness. As long as life is possible, even if only in a minimal degree, you should hang on to it, in order to scoop it up for the purpose of conscious development. To interrupt life before its time is to bring to a standstill an experiment which we have not set up. We have found ourselves in the midst of it and must carry it through to the end. That it is extraordinarily difficult for you, with your blood pressure at 80, is quite understandable, but I believe you will not regret it if you cling on even to such a life to the very last.[6]

He wrote that on the 10th of July, and on the 25th of July he wrote:

> It is really a question whether a person affected by such a terrible illness [the letter is about a woman who has cancer] should or may end her life. It is my attitude in such cases not to interfere. I would let things happen if they were so, because I'm convinced that if anybody has it in himself to commit suicide, then practically the whole of his being is going that way. I have seen cases where it would have been something short of criminal to hinder the people because according to all rules it was in accordance with the tendency of their unconscious and thus the basic thing. So I think nothing is really gained by interfering with such an issue. It is presumably to be left to the free choice of the individual. Anything that seems to be wrong to us can be right under certain

circumstances over which we have no control and the end of which we do not understand.[7]

Suicide, prematurely breaking off the experiment of life, is hardly compatible with the demand for ever greater consciousness inherent in the Jungian concept of individuation. And yet no one can prove that suicide may not be the very goal of an individuation process. We cannot presume to pronounce whether a given suicide is right or wrong. But the position we take toward suicide will influence how we deal with suicidal persons.

Therapists are regularly involved with suicidal potential in a variety of forms. In analysis, suicide as a theme is intimately related to the theme of transformation. These two themes often appear together when change is slow to occur; a feeling develops that radical means must be employed to hasten things along. But the theme of suicide also arises in an analysis when the question of the meaningfulness versus the meaninglessness of life becomes relevant. It is a theme that must be touched on at some time in the course of any longer analysis. It does not necessarily call for the implementation of a crisis intervention, unless of course it takes the form of a crisis.

Then again the theme of suicide is always present in our work with depressive patients. There are no depressions in which it does not play some part. When things are calm, I find it meaningful to discuss with the patient what is to be done if suicidal impulses become overpowering. I believe that clear agreements should be made about what the therapist is and is not willing to do, about the conditions under which hospitalization would be indicated, and how this would be executed. This is not crisis intervention, but crisis prevention: suicide is discussed, the act is recognized as one that can be used to threaten, and clear agreements are reached in the event the situation arises. This is helpful for many persons. Those absolutely bent on taking their lives will do so in spite of such precautions, and in the final analysis no one can take responsibility for a suicide except the suicidal person.

Crisis Intervention on the Telephone

Crisis interventions before suicide attempts are often conducted over the telephone. In his comments on the crisis hot line, Leutwiler finds the telephone ideally suited for crisis interventions with suicide threats.[8] The special setting of the telephone, where one is not seen, keeps the threshold of contact from becoming uncomfortably high. Anonymity can be retained, and the hot line is available at all times, staffed around the clock. One often hears from emergency psychiatrists that the last thing persons threatening suicide want is a visitor; what they do want is just to be able to talk with someone. A suicidal person who telephones, though, has not only destructive impulses but also the mild hope of being helped.

The ground rules for such telephone conversations are to maintain contact and to win time. Suicide is an act of impulse, and what counts is getting beyond the critical moment. Persons contemplating suicide cannot imagine anything changing, or that time could make any difference. If time can be won, it is quite conceivable that they will begin talking about their problems, and it may be discovered that a recent wounding has triggered the acute crisis.

The following example does not come from a crisis hot line, but from my own practice. A young man, twenty-eight years old, an analysand in therapy with me for some six months, called me around midnight to tell me he was about to kill himself. To my question "So what is it this time?" he responded at length. The phrase "this time" not only revealed my aggression in the face of a suicide threat, there was also a story behind it. Both the analysand and his wife had already made several suicide attempts. Both had used their suicide attempts to manipulate each another. Both were well informed about medications and knew how much one can take without causing irreparable damage. Since these scenes had repeated themselves with a certain regularity, it was difficult to keep the gravity of the situation in mind. This background came to expression in my intervention, in spite of which the rule holds that those persons who have made a number of suicide attempts are especially endangered.

The analysand did not take my intervention amiss. He was highly inebriated and told me he had had an awful day, had gotten angry at work, and had had a conversation with his former wife about money which he did not have. Afterward, out of anger, he had bought an audiocassette player which lay far beyond his financial means. He was the sort to buy something when he felt bad, hoping by means of the new object to enhance his worth and cheer himself up. Unfortunately, he was already in a tight financial spot, and now he had bought himself an unthinkably expensive machine, more than three thousand dollars worth—a component that raises one's status in a highly narcissistic manner. Theoretically he knew that his need to buy became obsessive whenever he failed to face up to his anger. Whenever he admitted his anger to himself and expressed it to others, this need to buy did not rise up. He had tested this successfully on several occasions. He must have been angry with himself for backsliding and upset with himself for being so angry. In any case, he went drinking in the evening. When he arrived home late, his wife wasn't there. A note lay on the table informing him that she had gone out with a male friend. He went looking for her and found her, appearing just in time to see her dance a tango with the friend. Horribly jealous, convinced that his wife would leave him and that the friend would cheat him, he decided to kill them both first and then himself. He would do it with a revolver, which he would first have to procure. Then he remembered that he must first call me, on account of the agreement we had made in case of suicidal intentions.

We had agreed that he should call me before making a suicide attempt in order to be sure that this was what he really wanted. So he called me and told me everything. I listened and posed some questions. He was difficult to understand, as inebriated persons often are. I affirmed, repeated, and underlined his statement that it was really asinine for him to have bought the tape player. Looking back on it, I said, could really make one angry. But I also found it understandable that he would react with the old pattern of behavior, given the depth of his anger. Here I was inviting still more anger from him. Yet I was also making him feel understood and giving him the sense that I grasped what a precarious situation he had gotten himself into. From time to time he swore that I could not stop him from committing suicide and would not tell me from where he was telephoning. I replied that I would not hold him back from suicide; we would only talk. We just had to get clear on a few things. Then I also asked him how he wanted to kill himself.

Suicide research has established that situations in which persons already know in detail how they plan to kill themselves are more dangerous than those in which they still have only a vague idea. To my question, my analysand answered that he had enough pills. I asked him if he was not afraid of a choking reaction (he had informed me that, during his last suicide attempt about a year before, the pills had caused violent choking and vomiting). He replied that he could tell me in our next analytical hour if the pills had made him gag. Here I intervened very decisively: no, he would not be able to do that; if he ate the pills he would be dead as a doornail. There was nothing more to discuss. A long silence followed, during which I heard from his breathing that he was still on the line. Then he suddenly began complaining about his wife, about his former wife, about her plan to extort all his money, about how all women played evil games with him, all of them as a group. I listened to him and asked him in each case simply to be more precise by telling me *how* they had played dirty with him, supporting him as well in his complaints. "Maybe I can take the tape machine back or sell it again," he interjected. I began to feel a little better. He added that he would have to talk with his wife. He wouldn't tolerate such notes. "Is that honesty or sadism," he asked "when someone leaves you such a note?" He talked a long time about whether it was honesty or sadism, or what else it might be. "Oh well," he suddenly concluded, "I'm tired now. I'm going to bed."

Obviously his problems had not yet been solved, but he did have an idea about how to approach them. In the following therapy hours we were able to discuss matters calmly, including the wound signified by the note his wife had left. We discovered that his former wife had also left behind a letter for him on a table, a letter that marked the beginning of their separation. The current note on the table touched off his separation anxiety, which had been accumulating ever since.

According to Henseler, one often finds a common denominator between the pre-cipitating situation of a suicidal crisis and traumatic situations from an individual's biography.[9] As a whole, such a crisis is so large that it can hardly be named. An intervention must break the composite crisis down into its component crises. In this way, the man in our example was allowed to voice and distinguish between the various angers he had experienced during the course of the day. Then he could feel his despair being accepted and taken seriously. He could sense that his wound had at least received a hearing, even though we clarified it only later. In this crisis intervention by tele-phone, it was unusually fortunate that I already knew the person on the other end, since a tricky aspect of telephone contact is the lack of a safeguard against being cut off at the other's will.

Looking deeper into suicidal crises, we usually find a number of unresolved crises piled on top of each other. One day a straw breaks the camel's back. Often minimally integrated socially, many suicidal persons have experienced severe psychic hardships in early childhood. They live in a state of massive self-alienation. They suffer from an aggression syndrome such as the congestion or turning inward of aggression. But in regard to aggression a collective dimension is also involved: nations with higher murder rates experience fewer suicides. America has a very high murder rate and a comparatively low suicide rate, whereas in Austria we find the exact reverse. According to Ringel, Austria has the highest suicide rate in all of Europe, which in his estimation is the result of aggression turned inward, a socially promoted tendency in certain countries.[10]

Further, most suicidal persons have a high-strung ego-ideal, a severe superego exacting high standards. This means that they have grandiose fantasies accompanied with a corresponding inferiority complex. They tend to flee from unbearable situations.[11] Pill, drug, and alcohol addicts are statistically more endangered by suicide than nonaddicts. Escaping into drugs and wanting to forget instead of wanting to get things together are typical features of the suicidal mentality. This is due as much to the inhibition of aggression as it is to grandiose ideas that tolerate no failure. Suicidal persons are often contagious, as is evident from the peculiar phenomenon of school-wide "suicide epidemics" in puberty and adolescence. Under certain conditions, inspiration for suicide may also derive from literature. Goethe's Werther is just one example of a famous literary suicide.

The Presuicidal Syndrome

Every act of suicide is preceded by the presuicidal syndrome. As described by Ringel, this syndrome is indicative for the prognostically and diagnostically important assessments of the degree to which a given individual is suicidal.[12] These assessments can in turn help us in our deliberations over the question of protecting an individual from him or herself. The presuicidal syndrome is also useful in crisis intervention, which should attempt to reverse the course of the syndrome. This syndrome consists of:

- — a narrowing trend,
- — a congestion or turning inward of aggression, and
- — compulsive suicidal fantasies.

By *narrowing trend*, Ringel means that suicidal persons become increasingly restricted not only on various levels of their experience and perception, but also in their social lives. He points out that among these persons a *situational* narrowing trend usually takes place that renders many previously available life options no longer viable. They may suffer a loss of meaning in their relationships or at work, or a loss of work altogether. In addition, there is a *dynamic* narrowing trend: suicidal persons begin to have a one-dimensional perception of reality. They think one-dimensionally about everyday events and see only what minimalizes or idealizes themselves in a one-sided way. As a result, their patterns of behavior grow less numerous and less variable.

Their lives become increasingly dominated by a single affect, and their defense mechanisms are no longer modulated. Usually one or two defense mechanisms predominate: idealization and denial. Further, an *interpersonal* narrowing trend is usually observable in the form of increasing isolation and loneliness. Or suicidal persons make do with relationships that they devalue and which therefore mean little to them. This interpersonal aspect of the narrowing trend often remains hidden when they describe their relationships in unrealistically idealized terms, so as not to have to disparage them. Only when one asks oneself if they feel nourished and recognized does it become apparent that we are dealing with increasing isolation going hand in hand with increasing devaluation of available relationships.

Yet another area in which a narrowing trend develops is the *realm of values*. One by one, various spheres of life lose their interest. After a while, no values are left whose preservation merits the requisite investment of energy.

Ringel judges persons to be endangered by suicide when a definite and tangible narrowing trend approaches the critical point. This narrowing trend corresponds to a silent crisis of understimulation. It not only has an obvious affect on suicidal persons, but is at work in the background of every crisis. It is the characteristic feature of crisis, since it is the characteristic feature of intense anxiety.

The turning inward of aggression (the inability to mobilize aggression), which Ringel sees as another characteristic feature of the presuicidal syndrome, also belongs in principle to every crisis. It is telling that the suicidal fantasies arising out of this dynamic become compulsive with time. Far more prominent than the intention to kill one's self is the wish simply to have a break from the torturous life situation, to be allowed a nice, long sleep in order to forget everything. This is what distinguishes the suicidal crisis most importantly from other crises.

Developments Leading to an Act of Suicide

Henseler provides an explanation for the genesis of these suicidal fantasies.[13] His description of the dynamic of self-killing supplements the presuicidal syndrome as worked out by Ringel. Henseler describes the step from the narrowing trend, which marks every crisis, to the suicidal fantasies proper. He bases his view on the following observations. Biographies of suicidal persons show serious impairments of self-esteem. They are very labile, easily feel threatened, and quickly get the feeling of being abandoned, helpless, or powerlessness. All of this has a constricting effect on their lives, which can become even further constricted through experiences of failure. To offset their lability, they have a great need for power. If they suffer a wound, they deny reality in an attempt to keep their self-esteem from floundering, and bound up with their narrowness is a marked sensitivity to wounding, sometimes to the exclusion of everything else. Their denial of reality can take the form of idealizing themselves or their surroundings. Aggression is very often blanked out completely. This can be seen with particular clarity when suicidal persons are asked to write stories to accompany pictures of relatively undefined scenes (e.g., the Object Relations Technique

Figure 4.1
The Presuicidal Syndrome (E. Ringel)

1. Narrowing Trend

Situational:	Being overwhelmed by an overpowering, unalterable situation; not knowing whether one is "coming or going"
Dynamic:	Emotions which move in only one direction (despair, anxiety, hopelessness) without compensation
Interpersonal:	Isolation or devalued relationships
Realm of Values:	Devaluation of successive areas of life, which then lose their interest; realization of values no longer possible; one's own existence valueless

2. Inhibited Aggression or Aggression Turned Against Oneself

3. Suicidal Fantasies

- The wish to be dead

- Killing oneself

- Imagining how to do it

- These images become compulsive

---

test).[14] Here one notices how most conflicts are obscured in the stories they write. When a denial of reality, coupled with idealization, suffices to restabilize their self-esteem, they can begin living again—until they suffer the next wound.

When their denial of reality no longer suffices, however, fantasies of retreating to an original state of harmony follow. These fantasies are not so much concerned with the desire to kill themselves as to be able to leave it all behind in order to attain a harmonious primal condition. Suicidal persons ultimately lack a feeling of safety and security. For example, they lack the self-assurance that would give them the right to be angry without having to fear rejection. When they fear they are on the brink of a major breakdown, they turn their fantasies into deeds. Suicide may then be seen as the only creative deed remaining open to them.

These fantasies of retreat to an original state of harmony are mostly fantasies of peace, paradise, and beauty. Suicidal persons rarely consider the fact that return to the primal condition means death. When speaking with them, it is always seemingly unnecessary, but in fact essential, to make clear the point that after the suicide they will really be dead. A suicide's exit from life always has the character of an appeal. Invariably directed at someone, suicide is always bound up with a certain revenge.

Henseler's primary concern in crisis interventions with suicidal persons is to sound out the decisive wound that they have experienced and to talk with them about it. In

Figure 4.2
Developments Leading to an Act of Suicide (Henseler)

1. Self-Esteem Deeply Shaken	In the presence of an already existing narrowing trend (Ringel)
• Wounds	
• Disappointments (experiences of loss)	
• In someone whose aggression is already turned inward or inhibited in some way, feeling of anxiety (of being threatened, abandoned, helpless, powerless)	
2. Deployment of ''Coping Mechanisms''	Protection of self-esteem
• Denial of reality	
• Self-idealization and/or idealization of environment	
3. When Step 2 Is Not Enough	
• Fantasies of retreat into a harmonious ''primal state''	
4. Fantasies Converted into an Act of Suicide	
• Preempts the narcissistic crisis	
• Satisfies the need for revenge	

the process, the relationship between the most recent wound and an earlier traumatic situation can be brought to consciousness. In other words, the wound has struck them in a place where they suffer from an unconscious complex and where they are therefore especially sensitive. Ringel's concern is to reverse the narrowing trend that closes down the flow of life energy.

It seems to me that Henseler's and Ringel's concepts complement each other very well. It is just as important to discover the decisive wound as it is to find a way to stop the narrowing trend. From this perspective, we may judge a thesis going back to Freud and Abraham as therapeutically rather dangerous.[15] They suggested that the hate which suicidal persons direct against themselves (instead of the person who inflicted the wound) must simply be redirected toward the actual offender. But if we therapeutically stimulate rage against others, this may precipitate intense guilt feelings in persons with suicidal tendencies. These guilt feelings once again have the effect of injuring self-esteem and may force them to forestall a narcissistic breakdown by means of suicide.

It should to be taken into account in crisis interventions that the lives of suicidal persons, tossed back and forth between impotence and omnipotence, exert a characteristic influence on therapists, who sometimes feel powerless and at other times feel they must be all-powerful. Moreover, images of a primal condition of harmony will be transferred onto the therapeutic situation. Suicidal persons present a great demand for symbiosis, which they would not be able to stand in reality. If we try to direct their attention to inner images of primal harmony (e.g., by encouraging guided fantasy or painting), so that they may experience the security one's own psyche can provide, we may be answered with the accusation that the problem has been "swept under the rug." But years later the same person may well confess how essential it was for him or her to have been referred to these inner images.

A suicidal crisis, more than any other, requires intervenors to set clear limits and to make clear contracts with their clients. The entire life of a suicidal person is gripped by the crisis. Panic is absolute and is mediated absolutely to the helping person, although we often defend ourselves against it quite aggressively.

Crisis interventions made before or after a suicide attempt require—as do other crisis interventions—prompt consideration of possible instrumental aids. Many suicide attempts are instigated by outer problems that intensify a narrowing trend already worsening. For example, suicide attempts are common among elderly persons when their apartments are taken away from them. Fundamentally, they have a great desire to live, but they are so attached to their apartments that at the moment of losing them, it is as if the ground on which they stand is cut out from under them. Among younger persons, suicide attempts are often observed in connection with unemployment, separations, alcohol, and drugs.

Case Example

As described above, a crisis intervention works in two directions. We set out to undo the presuicidal syndrome, the narrowing trend, the turning inward of aggression, and the compulsive suicidal fantasies. And we attempt to lay bare the central wound, working our way toward the deepest meaning of this wound and the feelings associated with it. We must differentiate between the conscious event precipitating the act of suicide, the unconscious problem underlying it, and perhaps also an incomplete developmental issue.

A thirty-eight-year-old cheesemaker came to me accompanied by his pastor, who had incidentally found him in the forest trying out a branch on which to hang himself. He sat down morosely and said he hadn't wanted to come. There was no point in it. There was no point in anything. And besides, it was already late in the evening (it was about ten o'clock). He seemed closed off. I asked him what it was that had no meaning. "Just everything," he replied. "And there is no point in talking to you either."

I made repeated attempts to establish dialogue with him. He declined my advances. I felt his enormous helplessness, and I expected rage from him, but I could not feel it. He declined in a friendly way. I sensed that my aggression was taking the form of dull questions which made no sense to him. I stopped asking questions and showed him that I could put myself in his place: we had thwarted his intention, and he must be having a hard time tuning in to us.

To this empathic intervention he was able to respond.

"That's right," he answered. "Next time I'd better be more careful. But as long as I am already here, taking up your free evening, I *do* have something to say. I sure don't want to land in that situation again!"

Then he told of his unhappy love. He had been very fond of a young woman who had turned him down. Apparently, he had not perceived this, however. It seemed he had denied reality and overidealized himself. When I asked him to describe the young woman, he said that she had been quite brusque with him, always on the defensive. But then she had always been basically very inhibited. He had reinterpreted her reserved—if not overtly defensive—behavior in terms of his wishes. He had over-looked her signals of rejection, or else he had interpreted them as shyness, again denying reality. She did not accept the flowers he had offered her; in his mind this was only because she was in the presence of others, she was just shy. He was interested only in her and didn't even look at other women anymore. There *had* been a widow who was interested in him, but he put this girl first. He had given up all his friends for her and always tried to be where she was. To the question whether she had noticed this, he answered, "Yes, of course." She often got infuriated with him, but that was only because she was so inhibited.

His remarks made it quite clear that all of his relationships had gradually narrowed themselves down to this one more or less fantasized relationship with the young woman.

A silence followed. "Yes," I inquired, "and has this young woman moved away now?"

He looked at me in disbelief. "No," he answered, "she got engaged. I can't handle it. That's why I wanted to hang myself."

His wound had resulted first from the young woman's preferring the other man, and second from the fact that her engagement had put a stop to his denial of reality. He had to admit to himself that the girl he wanted so badly didn't like him at all, maybe even despised him.

I intervened next by expressing my sense of how terribly difficult it is to accept having made a mistake in becoming attached to someone.

He started to cry. Sobbing, he said there was really no point in anything any more. There was no point in working. He had gone into the cheese factory because of the better hours. But he didn't feel valued there, and there were no animals there—he had always enjoyed animals so much. Previously he had worked for a cheesemaker affiliated with a farm. There he had felt good; he had felt valued. Now he might have better working hours and better pay, but he had done it all for the sake of the young woman. Once he had wanted to start up his own cheesemaking business, but now that was out of the question. A wife would be needed for that, and the wife was out of the picture. To my question whether there were no others, he looked at me sharply and said, "No, no! Of course I know there are others—but none for me. She's engaged now, period!"

He had thought he could lease a cheese factory at some point; that would no longer be possible, since he had no wife. He got this across to me as if to say, "Are you ever dense!" Then suddenly he asked mistrustfully, "Would you actually stop me from killing myself?"

I replied that I found it very strange that someone wanting to hang himself in the forest at night had been discovered there in the act. This was probably a sign that life still had something in store for him. But I would not stop him from killing himself; that was his responsibility alone. I only wanted to help him clarify whether killing himself was what he really wanted.

He sat back, satisfied, and remarked, "Well, well, you find it odd that I was discovered?"

I affirmed this, and he said, "I've not yet looked at it that way, but it's true; it *is* odd." And then he sat up a little straighter, grew a little in his chair.

Next I asked him who should be shocked by his suicide. Naturally the girl should be shocked, he thought. She should have to pay for his suicide for the rest of her life. She should think of him with every slice of cheese. I replied that I did not believe she would really be able to keep that up her whole life. We are quick to forget.

What came to expression here is a typical fantasy of suicidal persons: not only do they imagine themselves in a state of peace, but they often imagine their funerals as well. They see the people who come to weep for them, feel guilty toward them, drench their veils with tears, and never recover, or at least undergo a wrenching upheaval during the funeral. I had destroyed this fantasy in him by saying I did not believe that the girl affected by his suicide could think about his death for such a long time. But he insisted that no one could forget so quickly. I asked him if he could remember the first girl who ever gave him a kiss. He thought for a long time, named a name, took it back, mentioned another name, and then was forced to admit that he couldn't remember.

"You see," I said, "even beautiful things are so quickly forgotten."

"But a suicide attempt is not as quickly forgotten as a kiss." He thought again. "Then there would have been no point in the whole thing," he said.

I offered the interpretation that, above all, he wanted to revenge himself on the girl. By preferring the other fellow, she had wounded him, I suggested, especially considering how much he had already put into the relationship.

I did not yet mention the unreality of the whole relationship. He looked at me appraisingly in response to my intervention. "You make me look like a guy only bent on revenge," he said. "You shouldn't treat me like that. You shouldn't talk to me that way. I'm a good loser! As far as I'm concerned, she should be happy. The other fellow isn't worth anything anyway. But then after the divorce, she'd better not think. . . ."

"Yes," I affirmed, "she'd better not count on that."

"No, no way," he reiterated. "I'm no Pestalozzi and I don't care any more." (Pestalozzi was known for his extraordinary charitableness.)

An interesting change took place here. First, there was a narrowing down to the single aspect of revenge. I addressed both his need for revenge and his wound (which he was not going into at the moment). But I also acknowledged his right to revenge. This made it possible for him to show his generous side. His generous side was obviously connected in turn with self-idealization and disparagement of his successful rival. His prediction of divorce afforded him a further degree of self-idealization and disparagement of the other: the young woman's misfortune was already his good fortune. Referring to the dynamic of killing oneself as portrayed by Henseler, we can see that the intervention made it possible for him to take a step backward (from Step 3 to Step 2 in Figure 4.2). Here the crisis intervention in a stricter sense had come to an end.

He also made this step backward possible by taking, of his own accord, a "travel in time," that is, by contemplating what the future would bring. The narrowing trend was thus already slowed. The travel in time, a technique employing imagination, is well suited to crisis interventions, not only those dealing with suicide.[16] The idea is to bring a person to think about how things could look in half a year, a year, five years. For it is the nature of a crisis that, from within, the reality of passing time seems to be suspended altogether. If we can succeed in making the person in a crisis aware again of the dimension of time, then the narrowing trend can be stopped. One actually seduces them into a future that they do not believe they have. Without a future, we cannot allow ourselves to hope. To speak of the chance hidden in every crisis is a seduction into the future, into life.

After idealizing himself and disparaging his rival, thereby temporarily stabilizing his self-esteem, he said, "I don't want to talk about her anymore. I don't care about her right now. Now I have to think about me and how to solve my problems—one thing at a time." This was typical: the moment he could again idealize himself and devalue the other, he could think gratifyingly of himself; now he *wanted* to think about his problems. I asked him which problems he wanted to solve first.

"I have to get another job. I have to move away from home. . . ." On account of working in the cheese factory, he had been living at home again. Then, filled with fear if not panic, he exclaimed, "My God, everyone at home—they'll never let me out of their sight after giving them such a scare. They'll think I'm crazy, they'll want to put me in the mental hospital."

Here he began to get a sense of what he had done as seen through the eyes of others: what he had done was "crazy." He turned to me in fright, "Do you think that, too?"

I asked him how he would judge his condition. He thought it over. "The worst of it is over," he concluded. I affirmed that I saw it that way, too.

We decided that he should talk with his parents. This made him very nervous. "I can't do that. When I'm with my parents, I can't get a word in edgewise. And I can't think of anything to say anyway. Before, I used to get drunk." About drinking he said, "You know, I just wanted to forget. Death would have been forgetting, too. I imagine that it gives you peace of mind. But now I don't really want to kill myself anymore. I think *we* can solve my problems."

Essential problems immediately came into view, problems that lay behind the situation precipitating the suicidal act. First, he seemed only minimally detached from his parents; he couldn't speak with them and couldn't get a word in edgewise, was still acting like a small boy. And an alcohol problem was at least suggested. One could see that he was someone more likely to flee from a difficult situation than to find words for it. This was also clear from his desire to include both of us in the solution of his problems: *we* could solve them. I pointed out to him that the pastor and I would make an effort to help him solve his problems, but that it would essentially be up to him to find the strength to solve them. I told him I had the greatest confidence that he would be able to solve his most important problems. Then we discussed the order in which this should be done. He wanted to find a new job, to move away from home, and to consider more seriously the widow who was interested in him and learn to behave differently with her. Apparently he had made some blunders with her. He also wanted to lease a cheese factory and thought we should explain everything to his parents.

It was typical of him to draw up an entire catalogue of problems that was clearly and hopelessly overdone. Now he wanted to tie up all the loose ends in his life as quickly as possible. It was hard work bringing him back to the strategy that he had suggested and I had strongly supported, namely, to solve one problem at a time. His idealized aspiration was for us to do everything all at once.

This case again illustrates how a great number of problems get piled up and come to a head in a crisis. Hence the desire for all the problems to be solved simultaneously, in one fell swoop. In a crisis intervention, one should avoid being seduced into this kind of problem solving. Persons in crises usually present a number of problems. It is important to clarify which of them is calling most urgently for a solution.

We began by speaking with his parents the next day at three o'clock in the afternoon. He slept overnight at the pastor's home. His parents were notified the same evening. Their response was striking. They reacted first of all to his decision to move out and have his own apartment. They said right away, and kept repeating themselves, "But you are so inept in life—you can't move out! And now you've even made a suicide attempt. That settles it; now you must definitely stay!"

I told the parents that it almost seemed to me as if it were just fine with them that their son had made a suicide attempt; now they would be justified in keeping him at home. They glared at me. They probably thought I was a little strange. I felt a lot of anger over this attempt to badger their son into a juvenile position, and I voiced it, too.

Coming from these parents was an extreme narrowness, and they displayed a marked inability to empathize with their son's desires. It stood to reason that the cheesemaker needed both the pastor and me just to explain to his parents what was the matter with him and what he wanted to do. He and his needs were simply disregarded. His parents were totally focused on him, without being at all sensitive to

him. This could be the common denominator (Henseler) between previous and present wounding situations.[17] The young woman's insensitivity to him was salt in a deep,
old wound.

Not only narrowness, but also a peculiar, inward-turned aggression came from these
parents. During our talk they suddenly decided that it was better for him to have
wanted to kill himself than to have shot the poor girl. Apparently they had the
aggressive fantasy that he could have shot the girl as well. The pastor responded that
no one had said anything about shooting the girl.

Suddenly they began to moan about how dreadful it was to have a son who had
contemplated suicide. Now they would start contemplating suicide, too, for they could
not get over the disgrace. They quaked at the thought of "this disgrace" becoming
public. There were, however, no grounds for such a fear, since the pastor and I were
the only ones who knew anything of the event. But their fear showed that a rigid
superego loomed over this family embodied in "what they will think."

We concurred with the family that their situation was very difficult, but also
suggested that many long-standing problems could now be addressed. They scarcely
heard a word.

Hefti has pointed out that the family of an individual with suicidal tendencies
displays the same problems and psychodynamics as the suicidal family member.[18] We
can see this here in the narrowing trend, the aggression turned inward, and the need
for self-idealization. It prompts me to question whether narrowing may not be something one learns in childhood.

I appealed to the parents to recognize their son's urgent desire for a relationship
with a woman. I could well understand their sadness and their feeling of being left,
should their son move away. But they should try to tolerate their feelings of grief
rather than make their son feel guilty. If he felt too guilty, he would not be in a
position to find a woman for himself.

Since both the pastor and I had the feeling that this family urgently needed someone
to look after them, we asked a social worker to take the case. We were both too
identified with the cheesemaker to stand much chance of dealing profitably with our
rage. Moreover, it seemed to me meaningful for the family to have someone attending
to them for their own sake.

The real crisis intervention with the cheesemaker occurred during his meeting with
me and during the talk with his parents, in which with our support he could at least
propose what he intended to do next.

A loose arrangement for his care followed. I saw him once a week for a month.
Then he came approximately once every two months to discuss problems. We focused
on his new job in connection with his new apartment, and after a while on his
relationship with the widow as well. Relationship problems came increasingly to the
fore. His strong tendency to be disappointed developed into an overt problem. He
tended to be insensitive to what others were really feeling and saying, convinced that
the other person felt exactly as he imagined. He was demonstrating behavior that he
must have learned in his family. All the problems he had had with the girl repeated

themselves, as was to be expected. I experienced his strong tendency to be disappointed as quite dangerous, because it could have led to another suicide attempt. I made him aware of this danger.

From then on we talked less about suicide, and more about alcohol. He said a number of times that it was indeed a good sign that fate had sent the pastor to him. It made a huge difference once he realized that problems can be talked about and clarified by means of verbalization.

At first, he clearly had high hopes that we would take his problems away. He seemed to me like a child who had at last found people to help him, people to whom he could show what had to be fixed, right away. He turned to us filled with trust. But the theme of breaking away from his parents—taking the step from child to autonomous adult—was long overdue.

In this crisis intervention, it was actually possible to reverse the course of the presuicidal syndrome. The pastor was and remained a crucial support. In the beginning the cheesemaker always needed to have the pastor accompany him to the sessions. Sitting in silence, the pastor hardly ever intervened, but I think he represented an important reinforcement for the cheesemaker as an alter ego promising protection and support.

After a while, one noticed the repetition of a typical sentence in our talks: "Then I thought about what you would say, or what the pastor would say." The cheesemaker could thus integrate our counsel—and also ourselves as persons—into his system. We were "transitional parents" for him.

It seems essential to me in all crisis interventions with suicidal persons to find others who are reliable and who really walk together with them.

Only in the beginning did the cheesemaker transfer the fantasy of omnipotence onto us. Subsequently he was quite satisfied with a step-by-step solution of his problems, although he did tend to want too much. He overtaxed himself as a result of his idealizations, and so always failed to a certain extent. This naturally disappointed him. Wanting too much resulted also in part from his conviction that he was still lagging behind in matters long since mastered by others and from his consequent impatience for everything to happen without further delay.

It was important to confirm his progress and at the same time to explain to him that not everything happens so quickly. He needed to be reminded that he should not be so demanding with himself.

When a crisis intervention with a suicidal person is successful, the real crisis behind the suicidal impulse is uncovered, and the opportunity within the crisis can be identified. However, many suicidal crises run their course in silence and end in death. It would be a fantasy of omnipotence to suppose that all suicidal persons could be helped with a crisis intervention. Suicide is a reality with which we have to live.

Chapter 5

Mourning

Losses of every kind are the principal events that precipitate crises.[1] The loss of an intimate partner triggers a very particular kind of crisis, a crisis enveloping one's entire existence overnight. The loss shatters one's identity; one suddenly becomes strange to oneself, and the world outside becomes equally incomprehensible. In the process of mourning we have to take the communal self that we have built up with a loved one and reorganize it around a private self. Depending on the function the departed person had assumed in the life of a survivor, a certain quality is missing. The lost partner may have stood for security, excitement, encouragement, or guardianship, or something else.

This phenomenon moved Lindemann—the first to concern himself with crisis interventions in connection with mourning processes—to understand and implement crisis therapy as a therapy of substitution.[2] To this end he attempted to uncover what function departed persons had filled in the lives of their survivors. Then he either assumed these functions himself or instructed the patients' physicians to do so. This is what is meant by substitution therapy. Obviously it can reduce the initial shock of the crisis. Nevertheless, in my opinion the ultimate goal of a crisis intervention should be coming to terms with loss, not simply seeking a replacement for the departed person. Lindemann does indicate that, in a later phase, the psychodynamic of the survivors must somehow change so that they can better endure their loss. But this seems quite vague to me, and I think that if a substitute has been offered in the first place, it will be very hard to give up later.

Crisis interventions with crises of mourning in therapeutic practice seldom take place immediately following the loss itself. Usually they take place only after some time has passed, often in connection with crises concealed in psychosomatic illnesses; here the shock of losing someone is experienced decisively on the level of the body. This displacement unfortunately results in the actual precipitating event—the loss—becoming obscured. What often appear from the outside as only minimal hardships can send individuals into massive crises. Underlying these acute episodes of stress are crises of loss, which also explains the labile condition of the sufferers. They will often seek a crisis intervention when yet another experience of loss disturbs their laboriously attained psychic equilibrium, or when certain memories of the deceased arise.

We have our attitudes toward crises of mourning, as we do toward every other kind of crisis. We fear losses; we fear the adverse effect they have on us. We often avoid persons in mourning, for they remind us of death, of the fact that relationships can be broken, and that our lives can become miserable overnight. We feel helpless in the face of loss. Mourners are regarded as demanding in the interim immediately following their loss. Unconsciously they ask for something no one can give them: the return of their beloved. They have to focus intensely on themselves in order to get through their crises.

Reacting to persons in crises of mourning, we may persuade ourselves that, since little can be changed anyway, we must put our faith in time, which "heals all wounds." We sweep mourners under the rug with this attitude. Or because we feel helpless, we attempt to help, and then we run the risk of depriving persons in mourning of their independence. Needy and confused, they are usually very friendly and grateful for any help they can get. But when they don't get "better" (under these circumstances they can't), or if they gradually transfer onto their caretakers the aggression that appears during one phase of the mourning process (e.g., by blaming us for the death, or at least for the depth and duration of the pain), we often cut off our efforts in disappointment.

This type of crisis, too, confronts us with our feelings of powerlessness and with our self-imposed demands to fix the crisis quickly, that is, with our pretensions of omnipotence. But it is death itself confronting us with the limits of our power, and death is no easy match.

If we accept death as an aspect of life with the knowledge that a loss can have a catastrophic impact, then we can accompany mourners on their long road. Accompanying means encouraging mourners to express and formulate their feelings in the fellowship of another person who empathizes, allows memories to surface, and accepts the prospect of a long journey.

The crisis intervention in a strict sense comes to a close when mourners start to feel that they have found a trustworthy companion, someone in whose company they can fully surrender to the crisis—in other words, when they have established genuine contact with the therapist. This is considerably more difficult to accomplish than it sounds, because mourners don't easily get involved in new relationships; many encounters may be required before they come into true emotional contact. Compounded with these rather collective countertransference feelings are our own various personal experiences with death and our own mourning processes, both with ourselves and with our intimates, all of which influence our feelings toward the crisis at hand. Countertransference feelings—or their defenses and compensations—also arise in us when we notice that our client's present crisis conceals an underlying crisis of loss. Finally, we may experience special emotions which indicate specific feelings that we have repressed in our own grieving processes.

The mourning process is a process which detaches us from someone we have lost and brings us back to living our own lives again. The detachment should unfold in such a way that what has been lived in the relationship with the lost person is not also lost but rather "ferried back" into life. Mourning processes are undergone when we lose someone close to us or when we become separated from someone meaningful to us. But they also occur in children when they separate from their parents and in parents when their children grow up and leave, when one loses one's job, etc. In its essential features, the mourning process always runs a similar course, which is not surprising since it is virtually a natural process encountered by everyone and often accompanied by dreams. A closer look at the mourning process brings to light a series of phases that are comparable to those in the creative process. These phases of the mourning process can be described, keeping in mind that they naturally blend into each other and repeat themselves.

I will now give brief descriptions of theses phases in view of their significance for crisis situations with persons in crises of mourning.[3]

The first phase is the *phase of denial*. This is the phase in which one has the feeling that one is only dreaming. The loss is a nightmare and cannot be real. All pain is cut off; one feels petrified. This phase can last hours, days, or weeks.

The first phase passes over into a second phase, which I call the *phase of erupting emotions*, characterized by a confusing muddle of conflicting emotions. One begins to experience the pain of the loss as well as rage at having been abandoned. Anxiety, anger, and guilt erupt, and one seeks a culprit for death. Even joy may be felt, joy that a new chapter in life is beginning. These emotions are often experienced all at the same time, in a confusing mixture. Since we live in a society in which it is difficult to give emotions their due, this phase is especially difficult to endure. The question is frequently posed whether what one is experiencing is normal. Sleep disorders are common in this phase, as is heightened susceptibility to infectious diseases. We are dominated by the thought that we must pull ourselves together. And we have special difficulty in admitting our feelings of rage over having been abandoned; but pain is seldom given free rein either.

A third phase follows—if the phase of chaotic emotions has been suffered through and sanctioned. In this phase one begins to integrate the life shared with a departed person into one's own life. I call it the *phase of seeking, finding, and separating*. We hear from individuals undergoing this phase that they can't think of anything other than the departed person. This is exactly what they should do; they should think about the life they shared. They should let it rise again in memory, reliving it in recollections. They should enjoy the good times, and they should look for problems hidden in the bad times. But they should also—and this is the essential aspect of this phase—discover what the departed person brought into their lives, what that person brought to life in them, what his or her love engendered out of them.[4] I have concluded that those individuals who are aware of what in themselves was animated by their partners are best able to come to terms with their losses. For what has been brought into being through love abides in us. It does not disappear with a loss, however bereft the loss may leave us. In this third phase it is also important to discover what we have projected onto departed persons. What did we see in them that actually belongs to us? What have we delegated to them? What burdens have we imposed on them? For what must we reassume responsibility?

If we manage these tasks, the fourth phase of the mourning process follows. This is the phase of moving back into the world and relating to others again. Here one must finally let go of and "sacrifice" one's pain over the death of the departed person. There are individuals who hold onto their pain in lieu of the deceased. Having undergone a process of grieving, mourners approach others in a highly contradictory fashion. On the one hand, they want to form relationships with more feeling and more openness in order not to miss anything, for now they know that a partner can die or go away. On the other hand, they fear relationships that are too intimate, because they know the price of grief should the relationship come apart. The first relationships are cultivated in the tension between this desire to be intensely related, to live and love against death with all one's power, and the reluctance to bind oneself again completely. Often added to this tension is a bad conscience over abandoning the deceased. This bad conscience is usually soothed by a dream. It is typical for these phases of mourning to be accompanied by dreams. Dreams often escort us emotionally from one phase into the next.

We can see in the phases of the mourning process a model for overcoming serious crises in general. Emerging from a state of paralysis, we are again able to let ourselves be gripped by emotions. Then follows a phase in which the past wells up again into consciousness. We sort out what must be given up forever from what can be integrated into our lives. Then we can return to life with new possibilities for living and acting.

The process of mourning thus also exemplifies how a crisis—indeed a very serious crisis—is simultaneously an opportunity. Having completed this process, we gain new self-understanding, and we are often in better contact with our emotions. We emerge with new behavioral and relational possibilities, as well as a feeling of competence in dealing with crises. The feeling of being able to deal with crises becomes an essential aspect of self-confidence. The following is an example of the process of mourning.

A nineteen-year-old student in the final year of preparatory school (the *matura* class of a Swiss *gymnasium*) had lost his father two years before he saw me. Hans (as I call him here) was the oldest of three siblings and was sent to me by the school pastor for counseling. He was doing poorly in school. He seemed distracted and preoccupied. He had been shown a lot of understanding; a blind eye had even been turned to him since his father died. But now the period of grace was over. Hans would have to pull himself together; otherwise he would not pass the qualifying examination for university entrance, which would be absurd for such a gifted student. This was the briefing I received.

I was supposed to discover if there might actually be a more extensive disturbance involved. Tacitly, I was also commissioned to make it clear to this young man that he would no longer receive special treatment.

A very pale, lanky young man came to see me. He seemed preoccupied as he sat down and spoke very rapidly. "I'm at the end of my rope, but I can't come to therapy. I can't concentrate anymore. I can't sleep. Sometimes I sleep only an hour or an hour and a half a night, which is why I can't concentrate anymore. In the evening I am already afraid of not being able to sleep, and then of course I really can't sleep. But I

Figure 5.1
Phases of Mourning

Problems of Each Phase

1. Phase of Denial

- Loss of feeling, rigidity

One must continue as if this death hadn't really happened.

- Continuing as if practically nothing has happened
- Loss is cut off— emptiness
- Grief must be avoided
- Getting stuck in the following phases → chronic mourning

2. Phase of Erupting, Chaotic Emotions

- Pain, rage, anxiety, anger, joy, guilt, feelings → search for a culprit
- Restlessness → sleep disturbances, increased susceptibility to infectious diseases

The "emotional chaos" must be endured and expressed.

- Suppression of feelings in the emotional chaos that were not accepted—rage, guilt feelings
- The storm of emotions is tolerated only at the beginning of the period of mourning

3. Phase of Seeking, Finding, and Separating

"I can't think of anything but the deceased person."

- Deceased person is sought in dreams, fantasies, photographs, places frequented, stories → relationship is reestablished and often idealized

- The search for oneself is intensified while separation is avoided
- The loss is not accepted
- Pain takes the place of the deceased person

can't come for therapy. It would burden my mother too much financially. I can't do that. But I'm really at a dead end. I'm glad I can come to see you. At school they all think I'm learning nothing, or don't try. That isn't true, but nothing works any more. At first they thought it was the grief, but that's not it. I'm not down because of my father. The problem is that I am now the head of the family. [He sighed.] So much of what my father used to do, I have to do now. And I don't have time for anything. I can't be with my friends, can't be with my girlfriend. Sooner or later I'll lose her. It's

Figure 5.1 continued

- Confrontation with everyday reality (the need for affection, sexuality, help, etc.) creates new relationship

  "What function in life did the deceased person perform for me that I can reassume?" (withdrawal of delegation)

  "What did I hate or love about the deceased person which is at the same time a trait of my own?" (withdrawal of projection)

  "What did the deceased person awaken or animate in me through his or her love that abides and does not go away along with him or her?"

The deceased person becomes an "inner companion."

- Life options made possible by the relationship becoming one's own

- In this phase of remembering, problems in the relationship are identified and accepted

- The substance of a relationship becomes clearly tangible

4. Phase of New Relations with Self and World

- The loss is accepted

- The pain can and must be sacrificed

- The experience of being overwhelmed again by painful feelings can be accepted as a sign that we must again allow for memories of the relationship, problems, and positive encounters

- New relationships are lived in the tension between getting totally involved so that nothing is missed, and not getting involved at all to avoid having to suffer through the mourning process again

- The "departure complex" is not sufficiently considered

- The fact that the mourning process can be triggered again at any time is not sufficiently appreciated

---

all going to the dogs anyhow. The only reason I'm allowed to see you is because the school sent me. It can't be a burden on my mother."

I told him I had the feeling that he was under unbelievable pressure and that he thought there was no way out of his predicament.

"Yes, exactly," he replied. That was how he felt. It was good talking with me. There was no one else to whom he could tell everything. He couldn't burden anyone else. Then he asked cautiously, "But you I can burden?"

I assured him that I sensed both the incredible burden he was carrying and the feeling of not being allowed to share it, not being able to hand some of it over to anyone else. I told him I would be happy to help him carry the load; yes, he *could* burden me.

It was obvious that he was under incredible pressure and wanted to get out from under it. Right away he had named all the main factors weighing him down. And yet he asked—after having lightened his load a bit—if he could burden me with it. A transference probably took place here. He couldn't burden his mother, which made him feel that he couldn't burden anyone, including myself.

I asked him how he had experienced his father's death. He told me that his father had been sick for a long time, suffering from cancer of the large intestine. The family had done a lot of "grief work" (*Besorgnisarbeit*) with the help of the pastor who had referred Hans to me (the anticipation of mourning, loosely translated, is called grief work). They had discussed, for example, what it would be like when their father was no longer living. He must have made quite an impressive farewell, taking it all very calmly, according to Hans. He suddenly had a very good relationship with his father, who had even asked him to take his place to some extent after his death. Hans liked that. It made him feel important.

Hans was seventeen when he lost his father and was charged with the responsibility for a family. Assuming his father's position went fine in the beginning, he told me, but now it was too much for him. He hadn't been able to talk about it with his mother. She had gotten used to simply handing matters over to him, and Hans wanted to spare her the bother of it all. He sounded quite sensible as he said this. He spoke with a sober and studied voice that was in total contrast to the voice he had just used to talk about his stress.

Whenever he spoke in this studied way, I felt intense anger rising up in me. At first I explained it to myself as anger at the fate that would take a father away from his children, anger at the father, anger at the mother. I expressed it as follows: "Suddenly I feel intense anger. Do you feel anger, too?"

"Yes, yes," he replied calmly. He was angry, but one should not be angry. He had dreams. A bloody anger at his father reared its head in his dreams.

Now the problem was clear to me. Behind the acute school crisis was an unprocessed crisis of mourning. Moreover, in the phase of chaotic, erupting emotions, Hans had not allowed for anger. The presenting problem was evident: difficulties in school and the associated sleep disturbances. The school problem was highly acute, because he must not fail his final examinations. He must not fail because he must not disappoint his mother and because this would mean having to attend the same school for another year, which would mean having to stay at home another year. The pressure he was under would only get worse. If he passed, he would go on to study in another city. The pressure on this young man was enormous. Yet he seemed to be equipped to deal with stressful situations; otherwise he never would have made it through the previous two years. Now the crisis had come to a head. He also revealed that his achievement at school had already gone downhill before his father's death. But I believe this normal. High achievement at school can hardly be expected of someone subjected to such a stressful situation at home as the life-threatening disease of one's father. To achieve under such circumstances would require an enormous capacity to cut off one's feelings. That he was not capable of this was most likely a sign that he was close to his feelings.

He did not seem suicidal to me. The question of what resources were available for Hans also arose. Several areas of his life were only peripherally caught up in the crisis. There were his friends; but he didn't have any time for them. There was his girlfriend; but he didn't have any time for her either. Having no more time for his relationships seemed quite understandable to me, considering the fact that in addition to school he had to serve as head of the family. This involved speaking with authorities, negotiating with insurance agents, looking after repairs on the house, and supervising his brother and a much younger sister.

His circle of relationships had narrowed and was getting narrower. But they could most likely be resuscitated. An important source of help lay in his dreams, which he had mentioned at the outset. I decided to place my bet on his dreams. It also seemed important to get the mother involved in the crisis intervention. She needed both to be informed and to have the opportunity to talk about her grief. At the moment no instrumental helps seemed to be required.

I was sure that Hans hadn't really mourned. Although the entire family had done some grief work, such preparation does not replace mourning and can even abbreviate it. There is quite a difference between imagining someone dying and experiencing him or her as already dead. We experience the brutality of a loss only when someone is really no longer around.

Moreover, Hans's remarks to the effect that things had been very calm at the time of his father's death and that he had suddenly had a very good relationship with his father led one to surmise that previously there *had* been tensions, tensions which disappeared at the time of the illness. The ventilation of mutual rage would theoretically have belonged to the grief work. But the ventilation of rage is exceedingly difficult for persons in such a threatened position, and here it most likely did not happen.

As I formulated his situation to Hans, I did not see his sleep disturbances or his school crisis as his main problem; these were after-effects. Rather, I felt he had not yet given ample expression to his rage in the process of mourning his father. Another problem was his not wanting to burden his mother. While this was very considerate of him, it forced him to work everything out by himself.

I expressed my desire to work with him on the dreams in which he was so enraged. His sleep disturbances would disappear once his anger had received adequate expression. I also felt that his mother should be informed of our work or maybe she should even come to see me. But he should be the one to decide. I did not think therapy was indicated, but instead short-term counseling. I was convinced that he was strong enough to get back onto his own two feet again.

The remark that he would be able to sleep again once he had expressed his anger was naturally very suggestive. It was based on the experience that sleep disturbances belong to the second phase of mourning. Once this phase is past, sleep disturbances often disappear again. But the equation should not be rigidly reversed in order to insist that inhibited grief lies behind every sleep disturbance. There are, of course, other, totally different reasons for sleep disturbances apart from inhibited mourning.

Hans seemed quite relieved as I presented my brief theory. He promised to write down all his dreams right away.

He came to the next hour two days later. Accompanying him was not his mother, but his brother, two years younger than he. He assured me that what I had said the last time was true. No one in his family had ever voiced any of their anger at their father—not after he became ill, not before, and certainly not after he had died. Hans felt that his brother was in the same situation as he. His sister, he thought, was less affected by their father's death.

Now he told me his dreams of wrath in which his father appeared. Without any prompting, he acted them out, assisted by his brother. The first dream:

> My father is dead. I shake him; he should be alive! He does not come alive.
> I am furious with him.

That was a dream he had been having for the past two years, a dream which had plagued him all that time. During the session, he used his brother to show me how he had shaken his dead father, calling out in this psychodramatic scene, "Come alive now, come alive now!" At one point it became too much for his brother, who screamed, "Stop it already! I *am* alive!"

Hans said he didn't really understand why he wanted his father back, since life was actually better without him, apart from the fact that he was now loaded down with so many duties. Both of them agreed that it had been really lousy of their father simply to "take off" (they had basically experienced his dying as "taking off") and leave them behind to fend for themselves in their difficult life situation, with a sum of money that was less than adequate and a house that was more than expensive. Now they would have to see how they could work out what their father had gotten them into. The next dream:

> My father, down to skin and bones, is eating a big piece of meat. I ask him
> if he is going to give me some of it. He shakes his head and laughs. I scream,
> "You big ego!" He looks at me disapprovingly.

The two brothers acted out this dream psychodramatically, too. Each took a turn at being the father. This brought to expression Hans's considerable jealousy of his father. Father always got the best piece; it was his unquestionable right. Yet both boys felt very sad in the role of their sick father, gripped by the feeling that this piece of meat was the last they would get out of life.

Their identification with their father did not last long, however. The most prominent part of their experience was jealousy of their father, especially in relation to their mother. Naturally Hans's jealousy hinted at a desire to have his mother to himself, which explains why he was all too ready to take over the role of head of the family.

After his father's death, he did have his mother to himself. She even became dependent on him, just as she had previously been dependent on his father.

Hans wrote out an entire series of dreams. One by one, he and his brother acted them out. In each case, we tried to capture the feelings arising in both of them. The pitch of their confrontation with their father steadily rose until suddenly this statement rang out in the room: "Father was always an egoist. He didn't just start being an egoist when he got sick. He always wanted everything for himself; and when things didn't suit him, he always went away."

Saying this shook them both up. They asked if they were allowed to say such a thing. Both suffered a sharp twinge of conscience. I assured them that it was important to have it out with their father as they had experienced him—from his good side as well as from his bad side.

Hans responded, "I had a tough time with my father. I never loved him. I hated him. Of course, I know you aren't supposed to, but I hated him anyway. And sometimes I think my hate could have killed him. That's why I have to make up for it now. But actually I can't believe that my hate was strong enough to have killed him. I don't think I could have wished this disease on him. And besides, I never would have wished this disease on him. If anything, I would have had him die in a car accident."

I explained to Hans that unconscious death-wishes were a sign that he—as is typical in adolescence—had the wish to take his father's place. It was possible that there had been a strong rivalry between them, not only the usual competition between older and younger man, but also a rivalry for the mother. His death wish was an expression of rage at his father. He could not express it directly, since it is generally supposed that one may not burden a sick person. The theme of burdening, touched on at the outset of our contact, seemed to be a basic image of his problem.

This information calmed Hans. Without noticing it, we came into the third phase of the mourning process. We asked ourselves what the father had brought to life in the two sons. This is a very difficult question when the deceased was not a loved intimate, but an intimate who was simultaneously if not exclusively hated.

"Father always put me down," said Hans. "I always felt clumsy around him. I always did everything wrong. He provoked me to temper tantrums and then punished me for them—hard—by locking me in the basement. I still boil over when I think about how he provoked me and then punished me. To justify himself, he would always say that he wanted me to learn to deal with my anger. I wasn't allowed to play soccer, paint, or play an instrument. I had to do everything behind his back. He always wanted me to study."

His brother had a somewhat less problematic relationship with their father. "Father always wanted me to be grown-up. That was great on the one hand, because it made him treat me like a grown-up. But on the other hand, it was asking too much of me. I wasn't allowed to play soccer and couldn't do all of the things that Hans mentioned. He wanted me to study, too. But he explained to me that he himself had not studied enough, and that was the reason he was having such a difficult time now. He was so hard on us because he wanted us to have it easier later."

His brother's statement helped Hans to understand at least a little his father's harsh treatment of him. At the same time, in the work of mourning, a situation known from puberty was coming to life, namely, confrontation with the father, particularly with his negative side. Rage against the father, feelings of powerlessness in relation to him, and associated guilt feelings: together they tell an old story.

After a while the two came around to their father's good side. They were able to confirm each other's sense of how vastly interesting their father had been when he was telling stories, and what a bad temper he had shown when he was interrupted, which, of course, happened a lot with three children in the house. Yet if someone asked him to, he would start up again from the beginning, and then at some point he would get totally mixed up. Looking back, they could amuse themselves greatly over their father's peculiar talent, and they both hoped they had inherited this side of him.

By means of belated mourning, they made up for a long-overdue confrontation with their father. It is important to note, however, that although anger at the father kept coming out, Hans continued to maintain—even after he had expressed and experienced so much anger—that one is not really permitted to get so angry; they were, after all, "stricken by fate." This remark made a strong impression on me, and I felt it was high time to get the mother involved. It occurred to me that the boys had adopted this phrase from her, and there would be no getting at it as long as she remained outside the proceedings.

It turned out that the boys' new development had resulted in increased stress for their mother. Visibly happier, Hans was sleeping again. But he stopped taking over many of the tasks which he had formerly done without thinking twice. Naturally the boys reported at home what they had been doing with me in the hour. All of this irritated their mother in the extreme. It was not surprising that she felt mounting pressure and that she now had her own crisis. When a crisis intervention is carried out with a family member, it is not uncommon for the crisis to break out among the other members of the family as well, especially when they all share the same problem, such as mourning for a departed person.

One day the mother came to see me. Before sitting down she announced, "Now you see, the first thing I have to tell you is this: One does not say bad things about the deceased. And if you are doing that, then you are simply lacking in the necessary respect."

Taken aback, I waited until her state of being had had its effect on me. Then I said, "I understand that you are troubled."

She started to cry. Pouring out was the entire extent of her unresolved grief. "I am so mad at him for leaving me," she said and then listed the reasons why he shouldn't have been allowed to leave her. Of course, she knew he hadn't left her out of maliciousness. She knew that he would have been the last one to wish such a disease on himself, etc.

Thus she found herself in the position of having to say "bad" things about the deceased in order to relieve some of the pressure she was under. Her sons comforted her and told her they had been through it, too. They had been much angrier than she was; but now they were no longer angry with their father at all. This comment relieved her. She sensed that it was just this expression of anger at their father which prevented the boys from getting stuck in their anger, even bringing them to a certain understanding of him. I imagine that she finally used the example of her sons to guide herself, that they made her feel it was safe to express her anger and rage.

She came by herself to see me three more times. She discovered to her dismay that her relationship with her husband had been very difficult from the beginning, that it had been a mistake for them to get married, that they had not been right for each other. Memories were awakened of their life together, memories of times when he had wounded her deeply, and also of times when she had wounded him. The worst of it for her was that he had always made her feel totally unable to cope with life, unable to assert herself, and grateful for being taken care of. Her anger turned against herself as she said, "And I just believed all of it. I became more and more dependent. I let everything be taken out of my hands. And now here I am, so dependent. This is, of course, why Hans had to take over so much."

Only gradually did memories surface that revealed another side of her husband: a radiant and delightful man and a wonderful storyteller, able to "charm the birds off a tree." "And you see, because of these qualities, I could never leave him. It made me too attached to him." She repeatedly inquired, "Is it right? Can you admit to having scarcely loved someone? Can you admit to having hated so many things about him?"

At some point I said to her, "You should watch what you dream tonight. If you dream of your husband being bitterly angry, then we have clearly done something wrong. But then it would be my fault, because I told you to do it." She dreamed the following night that her husband approached her radiantly.

Now a practical matter in this crisis intervention could be addressed. The question of how much responsibility Hans should have at home had not yet been resolved. Must he do everything, or might she be able to learn certain things as well? He was prepared to hand over much of what he was doing and to acquaint her with those tasks. It wasn't easy for her to swallow this. The problem was not so much suddenly having to attend to matters which she had gladly avoided until then. What really bothered her was the feeling that her son was slipping out of her control. The oedipal problem from the mother's side now shifted into focus: her son was supposed to replace her husband. Although she had agreed to let him go his own way, she felt that his relationships with his comrades and his girlfriend were cultivated at her expense. She clearly saw that she would have to detach herself from her husband once and for all. And she also saw that she would have to let go of her eldest son, with whom, as she said, she had always had a very special relationship.

I then suggested to her that she make contact with other single mothers and fathers so that she could stop trying to satisfy her need for a relationship exclusively through her son. We talked one more time for two hours about detaching herself from her son.

Hans had one last dream, with which we concluded the crisis intervention after nine "hours of wrath" and five additional hours together with the mother.

Father is dead. He is buried again and I am relieved. We all go home. It is a sunny day. I leave with my friends. My mother is standing next to some man. I wonder if she has another boyfriend already. But then I don't really care.

The dream speaks for itself. The father is buried again. Appeased, he can at long last rest in peace, in the atmosphere of a sunny day. Now everyone can go home. But Hans's jealousy toward his mother's potential new boyfriend is already apparent. The large oedipal problem has clearly not been resolved in the crisis intervention; however, it has been addressed. Drawing attention to this problem and to the guilt feelings that inevitably accompany detachment from the mother can be a sufficient beginning.

Hans's sleep disturbances dissipated very soon, approximately after the fifth hour. In one of his "hours of wrath" he mentioned incidentally that he had a great fear of suddenly finding himself dead. Fear of dying and sleeplessness naturally have a lot to do with each other. It is the fear that one will simply die if one gives up control. We found a relationship between this anxiety, his guilt feelings toward his father, and the feeling of not wanting to live any longer under such duress.

Hans passed his qualifying examinations, went on to pursue his higher education, and found time again for his friends.

During a talk two years after the crisis intervention, he told me how immensely important it had been then for him to reduce the pressure he was under. He had experienced how new possibilities can be discovered by talking with someone, possibilities whose existence would otherwise have remained hidden. Having experienced the death of his father, he had the feeling that he had grappled with some crucial life problems and had even come part way toward mastering them. He was certain he wouldn't go under again.

This was a crisis intervention in which my essential procedure was to follow the lead of themes presented in dreams. Of course, it was unusually fortunate that the two young men had their own need to act the dreams out, which put them in touch with their emotional content. Dreams can offer extraordinarily important tips in a crisis intervention.

With young persons, a crisis intervention with subsequent treatment of the main problem has the added advantage of enabling them to get their lives back into their own hands again without unnecessary delay. And they don't get the feeling that a new mother or father is solving their problems for them, making up new rules along the way. Many therapies with young persons fail, in my opinion, because the autonomy called for at this age is not sufficiently encouraged. Crisis interventions can be more advisable in situations of stress than lengthier treatments.

What I find typical in this case of crisis intervention—which might have looked the same with an adult—is the phenomenon of a protracted crisis of mourning hiding behind an acute crisis. To be sure, Hans's belated mourning could have been much more comprehensive. But his detachment, as well as recognition of the complicated relationship he had had with his father and the fact of his loss, were accomplished even in this relatively short period of time. The feeling of being able to resume living with new competence was likewise palpable. In crises of mourning, the entire family is often involved. It was no accident that Hans brought his younger brother along, even though his brother was clearly less affected by the entire problem. Hans no doubt sensed that if the crisis were lifted from his shoulders, his brother might be the next one to take it on. He surely wanted to prevent this.

It is quite typical in interventions with crises of mourning for one family member after the other to make his or her way into the conversation.

In this case, the mother came to the ninth hour after the four weeks in which I had seen Hans twice a week.

Chapter 6

The Diagnosis of Life-Threatening Disease

The loss of health is also a crisis of loss which shakes us to the foundations and tears us abruptly out of the normal rhythm of our lives. Ill persons receiving the diagnosis of a life-threatening disease do not experience the crisis alone; their intimates, physicians, and therapists undergo a crisis too.

This precipitates a particular kind of crisis in therapists, a crisis whose main feature is usually the anxiety that they, too, could contract such an illness. This situation makes clear that disease belongs to life and can strike anyone. Our reaction to persons in this crisis depends on how much anxiety we have in regard to illness in general, on whether we can accept illness and death as part of human life or instead are convinced that they are to be avoided. There is, of course, also the more specific question of how much we fear particular diseases. In a group discussion of the crises of physicians and therapists in such cases, it became clear that those illnesses we suppose we stand a good chance of avoiding by living sensibly are not as anxiety provoking as are illnesses that seem less affected by lifestyle and break more abruptly into an individual's life.

Naturally our own encounters with various diseases in our own lives influence both the manner in which anxieties are precipitated and the manner in which we cope with them. Moreover, our own experiences with a particular disease can result either in a preoccupation with other persons who have the same disease, or in an avoidance of them. Whether we confront ourselves repeatedly with the disease or flee from it depends on the opportunities we have had to work through our reactions to it.

The loss of health, like every loss, must be mourned. Processing this shock, we once again encounter all the phases of mourning I have described in Chapter Five, with minor modifications. The person affected by the disease does not go through this mourning process alone; it is co-experienced in a somewhat altered form by both intimates and caretakers.

The Mourning Process and Guilt Feelings

First I will describe the loss of health from the perspective of the ill person.

Here, too, we have an initial phase in which the illness is met with denial; one does not want to admit "it." Ill persons live in shock. Seemingly sensible, they often agree to have certain operations and treatments without huge displays of emotion, for emotion is cut off at this point. Very often, later on, ill persons don't remember what was discussed in this phase; they feel as if the situation has run right over them. It may anger caretakers that their explanations and instructions were not heard.

As in the mourning process, the phase of denial is again followed by the phase of erupting chaotic reactions. Diseased persons are furious over their fate, protesting, asking themselves, "Why me? What did I do wrong?" They feel guilty. They ask themselves for what the disease could be a punishment, torturing themselves even more. The problem of guilt feelings seems crucial to me in this context, and it appears to be getting more crucial all the time. I will therefore take the risk of diversion to add some more detailed thoughts on the subject.

For some time now various writers have been advancing a new explanatory paradigm for health and disease.[1] According to this explanation—which is gradually being accepted by a wide spectrum of the population—body, mind, and environment work together in a dynamic equilibrium. This means that equilibrium is continually lost and must continually be reestablished. Confirming this principle, it can be observed that every living organism exhibits the tendency to organize itself according to a return to a state of equilibrium. Seen in this way, health is a dynamic equilibrium and disease is a dynamic disequilibrium, a transitional phase, a time of crisis, at whose end a perfect new equilibrium should be achieved. Yet this new equilibrium does not necessarily comprise what we normally understand as health. The acceptance of a disease and imminent death can also lead to an equilibrium.

Illness can thus be understood as an expression of unresolved physical, psychic, or social problems, problems that can also manifest themselves, either directly or through their consequences, in the physical, psychic, or social domain. Conversely, it is also true that psychological and social problems can be temporarily "resolved" by means of a disease. Disease at least affords affected persons a retreat, putting them in the position of being able to ponder their situation and care for themselves, so that they can subsequently tackle their problems with the help of new strategies. The difficulty here, however, is that interpersonal problems may not always be addressed where they occur; instead, persons affected by disease may first be left to deal with these problems alone, or the problems may be addressed purely at the level of the disease.

Of course, diseases should not be idealized either. It is important, if we take this new paradigm seriously, to accept that a physical illness is also an opportunity to bring a disequilibrium whose primary cause is psychic into equilibrium. We are familiar with this in the case of physical diseases with concomitant developmental crises.

But alongside such self-healing through disease, self-destruction is naturally also to be observed. We are determined by both life and death. It seems crucial to me that we see not only the self-healing tendencies of human beings, but also their self-destructive tendencies. Otherwise the impression may arise that we must only think correctly to make even death, in the end, conquerable.

The new psychosomatic perspective is beginning to win acceptance. We no longer dismiss the mutual influence of body and soul, the causation of physical disease by psychic pain, or the role of environmental factors. From this perspective, the body is no longer simply a machine brought to the doctor for repair in the event of illness. In sickness or in health, one's body is still *one's own body*, with which one lives in one's environment and of which one expects quite a bit: illness is also an expression of present existence. Through the disease, we can begin a dialogue with ourselves, with aspects that are at the outset quite removed from us. Illness is part of our existence, the existential experience by means of which we are confronted with our transitory aspect and with death.

From a depth-psychological perspective, the advantages of the new paradigm are considerable. According to such a view, human illness—which reminds us that we are transitory—is not to be delegated, but is to be assumed as the individual's own responsibility. In this manner, looking now well beyond individual persons dealing with their diseases, a collective tendency could emerge in which responsibility for human illness would be assumed quite generally and not only delegated to the specialist. This implies staying in caring contact with those very aspects of life that disturb and wound us (acceptance of the shadow). On the pragmatic level, this entails feeling responsible for the healing process in order to play a part in affecting its outcome. Transformation of the doctor–patient relationship is one of the first side effects. Patients no longer simply hand over their symptoms and bodies until they are well again; they join in the discussion. And since from time to time they may not talk about what they really should, they interfere and meddle in the doctor's business.

In practice, this is where the paradigm shift draws the most attention to itself, in my opinion. Patients feel that the disease involves them as persons and requires them to be active in order to recover, more active than simply obeying the doctor's orders. They want to graduate from the status of obedient inferior to that of equal partner. After all, the disease is something belonging to the patient. But patients rarely manage to contribute what they could and should: they do not succeed in asking themselves the right questions. When physicians do not manage to ask these questions of their patients, the patient's contribution does not make its way into the conversation. Instead, patients earn the title of "petty physician." Individual responsibility for the disease gets lost in mutual anger and distrust. One might have asked: What does this disease mean for me at this moment in my life? What message might it contain for me? How can I still feel as good as possible *with* the disease? Does it allow me a necessary quiet pause from life? Why would I need that?

We take a very positive step when we as individuals take responsibility for our diseases, understanding them as life's call to establish a more adequate equilibrium, or as a confrontation with the fact of *having to die*, of *having to exist while taking leave*. But the flip side of responsibility is the feeling of guilt. This seems to me a crucial side effect of the paradigm shift.

Increasingly I encounter, partly in connection with a group of therapists and physicians who discuss psychosomatic issues, but also in my therapeutic practice as well as in my daily life, persons who relate consciously to their bodies. They do not treat their bodies like galley slaves, demanding everything of them and giving them nothing in return. They pay attention to the messages their bodies give them and try to organize their lives in a manner that is somewhat less hostile to the body than usual. But they also attempt to solve their psychological and social problems and tend to be environmentally concerned as well. In spite of this, from time to time they, of course, get sick. They, too, get the flu and sprain their ankles. Even these minor illnesses have them asking themselves what they have done wrong this time in their lives. The illness seems like an error they could have avoided had they made fewer "psychic mistakes." Here the question arises whether the new paradigm really has what it would take to create a new relationship to the body and its potential for illness. Is the new paradigm going to be used to tune out the problem of the body even more effectively, resulting in an even more advantageous hold on fear of aging, disease, and death? Here responsibility would not be viewed in accordance with how one *deals* with disturbances of equilibrium, but rather according to how such disturbances are to be avoided altogether. If this does not work, guilt feelings are already on the rise. Justice has not been done to the demand to create for oneself the best of all possible worlds.

These harmless examples already show how deeply a fantasy of omnipotence can get mixed up with the new paradigm. Disease, and finally even aging and death, can be avoided by means of this fantasy. If the psyche participates so fundamentally in the causation of disease and has such a determining influence on our way of dealing with it, it follows that we should be able to control disease psychically. Proceeding again on the assumption—actually a very old paradigm—that human beings are capable of doing what they choose, we behave as if the will was much freer than it really is. Thus we act with the conviction that the psyche is much more compliant than is actually the case, and soon enough we find ourselves joining in on the refrain, "If only he or she really wanted it, it could be done." But since we are under the influence of a false assumption—a fantasy of omnipotence that readily links itself up with holistic ideas— we are trying to fulfill an impossible demand. Thus failure is preprogrammed and is of necessity linked up with guilt feelings.

Someone with a life-threatening disease is confronted much more urgently by the question of guilt. For example, there are those who abide by the old explanation that disease is visited upon us by the hand of God. They believe that sin is death's final cause. Stricken by disease, they cannot escape the conclusion that they are guilty. Old explanations for death and disease are not stripped of their power simply by virtue of a new paradigm's validity. They continue to exert their influence from behind the scenes. The new explanatory schema even intensifies matters in the realm of guilt feelings: now we no longer simply have the feeling of being "stricken by fate"; we feel as if the entire event of illness is also at least partly within the province of our responsibility. We do not get free from the idea of being *stricken by fate*, and, in addition, we are personally responsible for the fate we receive. Thus *guilt feelings are multiplied.*

Naturally guilt feelings always play a large role in the life of the individual, and the question then arises whether it is so wrong for so much attention to be suddenly drawn to them. Shouldn't we see this instead as a sign that guilt feelings—precisely along with the new paradigm—must indeed be brought to the center of attention? The point would not be to avoid them but rather to learn to deal meaningfully with them.

Whenever we speak of responsibility, some form of guilt feeling is close by. With guilt we indicate the failure to meet some responsibility. In German, the word "guilt" itself (Schuldigsein) can also mean that we assume responsibility for the causation of a process.

In psychology, guilt is distinguished from guilt feelings in order to indicate that feelings of guilt do not always indicate the presence of real guilt. The probability of guilt increases along with the increase in assumed responsibility. To put it differently, since we cannot take responsibility for everything—to do so would be to assume that we can keep everything under control—guilt is an inescapable dimension of responsibility. Even if we are convinced that we must take as much responsibility as possible, in order to maximize our power over events and minimalize our subjection to them, we still have to admit that we cannot take responsiblity for everything. This admission is also very much included in the new psychosomatic paradigm, which says that we exist within a social-psychological-somatic system that interacts with many other mutually interacting systems.

From this viewpoint, guilt feelings have the function of assigning responsibility, i.e., of making us see that we still have to embrace some essential thing as belonging within our sphere of responsibility. More simply stated, we still owe ourselves something of crucial significance for our lives (schuldig in German means both "in debt" and "guilty"). Guilt feelings of this type—existential guilt feelings—can then be seen as intimations of important possibilities in life.

Existential guilt feelings are easily translated into neurotic guilt feelings. We may not see our feelings of guilt as a sign of some new thing, or as a petition asking us to find a new way in life. Instead we interpret it as a sign that we have failed to do something. This feeling of failure can be lamented intensively and unproductively. The reinterpretation of an existential guilt feeling as a neurotic guilt feeling is bound to a static model of life, a model based not on the notion that the individual develops in stages, but rather on the ideal that everything should be perfect from the beginning, and perfectly lived ever after.

Thus it is often around unreal failures that guilt feelings cluster, failures that are fantasized or taken much too seriously. Nor are these omissions understood as occasions to rectify something, which would be the case with experiences of real guilt. Instead, thoughts circle in an unproductive manner around an imagined guilt. Psychic life gets blocked. One suffers from feelings of guilt, while missing the call of personal existential possibilities contained within them. It is difficult to avoid regressing to the position of a child who has done everything wrong while at the same time being the authority figure pointing the finger at oneself. Naturally we project such authority figures, seeing them in a God, a father, fate, or some overbearing official. Everything remains imprisoned in neurotic guilt: the aggression necessary to change life, the associated rage at having been wounded—wounded by life so to speak, the anxiety associated with the disease, and the fear of advancing impairment and finally of death. Three points seem important to me in dealing with neurotic guilt feelings of this type.

First it is necessary to address the rage precipitated by the disease and the anxiety associated with it. Then there are the existential guilt feelings and the positive function they perform in connecting us more essentially with our existence. It is crucial to see that guilt feelings are a part of responsibility.

The fact that guilt feelings are an increasingly central issue in relation to the paradigm shift mentioned above shows how central is the place given to the individual's responsibility. Dealing with the associated guilt feelings must therefore also be seen as a central concern.

This concentration on responsibility, bound up with feelings of guilt, points to a demand inherent in the paradigm shift. Personal growth and progress are becoming issues of great concern, while a fantasy of overcoming death lurks everywhere in the background. The researches of Beck, Overbeck, and others would shift our concern to quite a different aspect of illness, namely, the need to halt incessant obedience to the demands of living, the need to grant onself a moratorium until an equilibrium is reestablished.[2] To care for oneself, to spoil oneself, to take a break from demands, to allow oneself the experience of well-being—only in relation to these aspects of life will an equilibrium really be achieved, in my opinion.

The extent to which our power-driven and achievement-oriented thinking sets the new paradigm's agenda strikes and disturbs me, although I am aware that the paradigm can open up other avenues, too.

These aspects of the issue seem essential to me to consider, because the new social–psychological–somatic perspective includes an obligation on the part of patients, even in the case of grave illness, to deal as well as they can with the seriously ill persons they are. Their frequent misunderstanding of this requirement has them feeling as if they must attach all kinds of conditions to their recovery, just to satisfy some theory. If they are unsuccessful in this, they feel even guiltier; they have not carried out the prescribed exercises intensely enough, etc. This problem is frequently found among persons suffering from cancer: if they deal well with their disease, they tell themselves, they will survive. The desire to survive is quite understandable, but I do not believe the additional stress helps sick persons make the best of the time left to them. And none of us can tell how long that time will be.

The experience of guilt feelings and the way we deal with them constitute what I see as the central problem in the phase of erupting chaotic emotions that occurs during the process of mourning a loss of health.

Also appearing in this phase is a fear of life and a fear of death. These lead to feelings of powerlessness and despair, and in the extreme instance, to resignation. An operation resulting in bodily disfigurement compounds the offense. The loss of an intact body must also be mourned. An unscathed body is an essential aspect of our sense of identity and wholeness. This feeling of wholeness is now injured, and the feeling of injury is understandably taken up and carried by one's social environment. Very often, hasty consolations are offered: amazing plastic surgery procedures can replace a breast; or, one should be happy that the malignant tissue has been removed; or, it is a good thing that there are now good prostheses. But that is one matter, and grief over the loss of an unscathed body, fear about how one's partner will react to this body, uncertainty over whether one can even let it be seen anymore, are other matters. Also erupting at this time is grief over the loss of the future imagined for oneself. Suddenly, the afflicted know in detail all of the things they would have wanted to experience and arrange for the future. But there is often no more time left to do so.

If the emotions of this phase are given ample space and not excessively hampered by calls for reasonableness and bravery, the next phase of mourning can be reached: the phase of seeking, finding, and detaching. Individuals begin to recall what has come to pass in their lives until now. Focused on one's own life, this memory work includes the life shared with those important to us. The past takes on new meaning in the face of a potentially imminent death. The feeling that what has happened was important is the feeling that allows affected persons to open up to the future, to death or to life. This is the most essential characteristic of the last phase which I call, following the phases of mourning, the phase of new relations to self and world. Individuals learn what it means to live while taking leave, namely, to live without ever forgetting that one must leave this life behind, and, directly in this transitory face, to live as intensely as possible. Naturally all of us must live while taking leave, but this perspective is more immediate to those threatened by disease than to others. Here arises the question of the meaning of the disease.

Caretakers, in principle, go through the same phases as ill persons, especially the first two phases. The mourning process requires considerably less time, but it is necessary to process the shock that the life-threatening illness triggers in them. Moreover, it puts them in the position of being able to work with those they are helping.

Helpers, physicians, and therapists also suffer an initial shock. Not wanting to admit the existence of their patients' menacing disease, they trivialize it. Psychotherapists can, for example, distance themselves markedly from the results of their analysands' medical tests, since they are in the end responsible only for the soul. It is important to accept the fact that we resist admitting the existence of such a disease because of the threat we feel it posing to our own lives, perhaps not at the moment, but as a prospect that is now drastically being summoned to consciousness.

Therapists also experience the phase of erupting chaotic emotions. They can fend off their anxiety by means of rage, rage over a fate which allows such a disease to exist. Or they can allow for their feelings of helplessness. If they do not have to defend themselves against their feelings of despair and powerlessness, they can tune into the ill person's various emotional states without completely losing their overview of the course of events. The ill person then feels understood and in good hands.

Figure 6.1
Phases of Mourning with the Diagnosis of a Life-Threatening Disease

1. Phase of Denial

- Shock

2. Phase of Erupting, Chaotic Emotions

- Rage, protest: "Why me?"
- Guilt feelings
- Fear of life, fear of death
- Powerlessness, desperation, possibly even resignation
- The insult of a disfigured body
- Grief over the loss of a future

3. Phase of Seeking, Finding, and Separating

- Reflecting on what has been until now—and consenting to the loss
  - → in relation to oneself
  - → in relation to partners

4. Phase of New Relations to Self and World

- "Living while taking leave"
- The meaning of the illness

Before long it dawns on helping persons that they are still alive, that they still have a future and are not for now threatened personally. This awareness is usually first registered through feelings of happiness. For a time, the theme of living while taking leave will also be meaningful to them. They will learn by means of this situation, which is of such existential importance for the ill person, how precious is life in the face of death. Above all, they will fight for life, sometimes mistakenly letting death out of their sight.

These phases in mourning the loss of health can be experienced in the course of an illness, or they can crop up before an operation, upon receiving a diagnosis.

As an example I cite here the remarkable account of a woman who had the good will to make it available to me. It was disclosed to a thirty-two-year-old married woman, the mother of two children, on the occasion of a routine physical examination, that a hysterectomy, although not of immediate urgency, was imperative. She describes her reaction and the course of the next few weeks as follows.

> Since we did not want any more children, I was not particularly shocked by the physician's disclosure. I inquired matter-of-factly into the

medical aspects of the operation, decided during the same consultation that I would rather not put it off any longer, and made an appointment. Later the same day I called up a doctor friend who affirmed my resolve. Once having organized help with the household and supervision for the children, I saw no further problems of great consequence.

I awoke the next morning in deep despair. The operation took on for me the significance of a bodily disfigurement, an attack on my woman-hood. No longer would I be able to feel like a "real" woman. The next few days and nights were horrible. I cried and screamed and cried. Then I called the doctor to postpone the operation. I could not cope with the problem, could not accept the unavoidable.

Even the smallest domestic chores became huge efforts, and yet I tried to force myself—I feared I would go crazy otherwise.

One night I couldn't take the fear and grief any longer. I was over the edge, beyond the bearable. I had a feeling of collapse, of being somewhere "over the edge," no longer capable of anything. I wanted to call for help but couldn't find my voice; I tried to get up and couldn't move.

All of a sudden, everything was calm. Having ridden out the storm, my soul entered into a deep state of peace.

But then it started up in my body. I had no more fear of losing my mind, but I experienced what came next as a brute fight for physical survival. My heart refused to participate. I struggled with it, talked with it, coaxed it to keep on beating.

Then I must have fallen asleep or fainted. When I awoke the next morning, the entire fracas was over. I was "over the hill," and I had been lucky.

That night I had the following dream:

I am sitting in a car, but am not driving. We have to cross the Gotthard Pass. The driver drives past the loading station (in the winter, automobiles were loaded onto railroad cars to travel through the Gotthard Tunnel). He wants to drive over the pass, which I do not understand. We have only summer tires on and the road is completely iced over, not to mention the snowstorms and impenetrable fog. We are in danger of going over the edge at every turn in the road. I am incredibly frightened.

Then suddenly we are on the other side. The sun is shining. We are driving downhill. Behind us is a mountain peak wrapped in clouds, where the snowstorm rages on. But we are already in Ticino (the southern part of Switzerland with an Italian climate). I am amazed—it all went so fast!

I knew that the crisis was over, and I made a new appointment for the operation. Everything went smoothly, and I never had any more problems from it.

Described in this account is the sort of crisis one can plunge into after receiving the diagnosis of a menacing illness. The disease itself does not have to be described as absolutely menacing to have this effect.

At first she reacted in a very businesslike fashion. Emotions associated with the problem were cut off. She was in the phase of denying the disease.

By the next morning and during the next few days, all the emotions which had been cut off returned and determined her state of mind to such an extent that she feared "going crazy" if she didn't keep up with the usual housework. Housework seems to have provided the only structure that she could rely on during this phase of erupting chaotic emotions. She went through this phase with full power and then fell into an experience of peace, accompanied by a dream. Described once again very clearly is the creative leap that can take place when the crisis is at its peak. But this creative leap also marks the transition from the phase of chaotic emotions to the phase of seeking, finding, and detaching, climaxed here in the dream experience, where it is confirmed that she is in the midst of an extremely dangerous passage. Apparently the passage cannot be avoided. In the end it leads into Ticino and the sun. This dream image was able to reassure her and to give her the feeling that the threat to life would subside again.

This crisis and the creative leap out of it proceeded without intervention. If the diagnosis of a life-threatening disease makes a crisis intervention necessary, it is because the crisis frightens the affected so much that he or she is not able to deal with it.

Example of an Intervention

An oncologist called to inform me that he had a woman patient who was clearly in a serious crisis. She had been operated on for breast cancer. Medically, everything proceeded without complications. The operation had been performed three weeks ago, she had actually recovered quite well, and, physically, she was in fine shape. Now she was at home, where she had retreated and was refusing to join the company of her family. She was also experiencing veritable intimacy attacks during which she would not even let the children go to school. She was giving the impression of a very distraught human being, someone at the end of her rope. He had suggested that she see a psychotherapist, to which she replied, "If I need psychotherapy now, too, then I lose the last of my self-respect."

This was a very important sentence for me. The doctor had told her she would not be likely to require long-term psychotherapy; all she needed was some help now. We made an appointment for the next day, at her convenience.

Upon arriving, the first thing the woman said was, "I need you desperately, but if I need psychotherapy now, too, then I lose the last of my self-respect." This was the first sentence she uttered. Then she screamed at me, "And why don't you have cancer? You could have the damned cancer! How can you just sit there without cancer, when I have cancer?!"

I felt quite helpless in the face of this outburst, was not in the least prepared for it. But I could understand it and thought to myself, if I were in her position, perhaps I would scream like that, too. Still, I felt quite helpless, despairing, grief-stricken, and filled with sympathy. So I simply let her scream, and after a while she asked, "Why don't you scream back at me?"

"Because for me, screaming is not called for," I answered. "I am confused, I can understand your outburst, and I don't know why I don't have cancer and you do have cancer." All of her grief, all of her despair, all of her anxiety, was converted into accusations against the world which she hurled back at the world, and the world at the moment was me. "I sense your anxiety, your powerlessness, your despair, your grief," I responded, "and I am glad that you can express your rage. I am glad that you can protest."

Thus I interpreted my feelings during her outburst as feelings belonging to her as well, concealed in the scene she had made. Of course, this disease also evoked these feelings in me. She did not seem to hear my interpretation. "Why me?" she asked, "What have I done wrong? What am I being punished for?" And without my being able to intervene, she continued, "Could you come to terms with a deadly disease?"

"Clearly it would knock me flat, too, if I received such a report," I told her. "Of that I am certain. But I believe if I had cancer, I would follow the example of those who live through it. Yes, I would go through a crisis, but I would think of myself as a survivor."

She looked at me in disbelief, "Are you joking?"

"No," I responded. "There is after all a percentage of individuals who survive."

She looked at me again, "Yes, that is true actually. You are right. But that is neither here nor there. In the end, I am one with cancer."

The woman—I will call her Dora—regarded getting ill as being related to something she had done wrong, to some punishing authority, although as yet she had only hinted at this aspect of her situation. By asking me if I could come to terms with a deadly disease, she showed her need for a certain solidarity: I, too, should soberly confront myself with this grave question. She stopped competing with me, for now. It was even possible that she wanted to learn something from me. I gave her a completely honest reply, from out of my empathy. Expressed in this reply, without my consciously intending it, was the perspective that cancer does not necessarily have to run a deadly course, but can also be survived. She heard this message, but still insisted that the point was that *she* was finally the one with cancer. In response, I reaffirmed what was for her without question an incredibly distressing reality.

Then, unexpectedly, she asked me if I was annoyed with her for having blown up at me. Again I explained to her that I saw her ruptured state as an expression of her grief and despair, as a sign of her distress over not having any idea of how to cope with the disease. I assured her that this was perfectly understandable.

She relaxed a bit, sat back in her chair, and asked how much time I had for her that day. I replied that I had reserved an hour and a half. "I'm so afraid of this disease," she confided to me in a low voice.

Then we began to talk to each other, and I think the decisive event in the crisis intervention had already occurred. On the one hand she was able to scream and voice her feeling of outrage over the unjust fate she had to suffer; but just as important was having established emotional contact with me by finding a way from competition to solidarity. She expressed her surprise that she had never considered the possibility of surviving cancer. This gave her hope, but she did not yet dare put her faith in that hope.

This awareness of the survivability of cancer can at the beginning make it even more difficult for many cancer patients to deal with their disease. Cancer is a disease that does not allow one to prepare with certainty for life or for death, but forces one to prepare for both. We mortal beings should do this all the time anyway, and yet we do not, behaving as if life were the only possibility.

After our stormy opening dialogue, Dora then told me, speaking in a perfectly normal tone, that after her physical examination she did not really come to her senses until she arrived home. She had submitted to the entire examination as if in a trance. She was operated on much too quickly, without at all following what was happening. She discovered herself "operated upon": she woke up with one less breast. She had had no opportunity whatsoever to reflect on her situation, nor had she any chance to decide if she even wanted the treatment in the first place.

From her subjective point of view, everything had happened at a terrific pace. Actually, at least six weeks had passed between the first examination and the operation. However, the point is not objectively but subjectively experienced time.

"At home," she said, "I kept thinking that it just wasn't true. One day I would wake up and everything would be completely normal again. This cancer: only a bad dream to wake up out of. But now I see: I wake up and I have a scar. And I have to live with this scar. For me it is a huge wound. I simply am no longer beautiful. I am disfigured. I have withdrawn. I have moved out of the marital bedroom. I am withdrawing from my children, too. I feel like I'm contaminated. I can't get in touch with anyone any more. And I feel like they don't understand me any more. I'm not myself anymore; everyone has changed. I'm horribly afraid of dying. I'm adding up the pluses and minuses of my life. What was my life really all about anyway? I want my children around me. But on second thought, I don't want the children around at all. I consider whether committing suicide wouldn't be better than wasting away so slowly. The whole family is in despair. I'm starting to sort out my things. I'm starting to give my clothes away."

I must have looked quite shocked when she mentioned giving her clothes away, for she explained, "My husband gets really mad about this giving my clothes away. He makes a scene and says I can't just give away the clothes he gave me." This was a very understandable reaction on the part of her husband. Giving away clothes aroused his fear of losing her even more than the disease itself.

Dora was forty-two years old, married, with three children: two daughters, age six and fourteen, and a twelve-year-old son.

She gave the impression of someone who had long been held in check. Her problem spewed forth as if from a broken dam. She had not moved beyond the phase of denial for quite some time. One could also say that she had been able to repress the crisis for quite a long time. Then, when confronted with everyday life, she moved into the phase of erupting chaotic emotions, with rage and rebellion in the foreground. She expressed her experience of herself from within the crisis very clearly: "I am no longer myself." From this she concluded that others no longer understood her. Heading into the storm, she swung back and forth from perfect understanding of her children to complete rejection of them, broke off her relationship with her husband, gave away her clothes. This impulsiveness, finding expression in her outburst, had manifested itself likewise in her daily life.

I considered what sort of therapeutic help I could offer her. A relationship with a therapist can really make a difference for someone with a disease of this kind. When dealing with physical diseases, it is important to keep in mind the fact that getting sick is already a deep wound to one's self-image. In general, we are very poor at living with our diseases. We are so determined by the ideal of health that practically every sneeze is experienced as a major wound. How much more wounded we are when confronted with a genuine disease!

Dora had responded that she could not allow any psychotherapeutic help to be offered to her; seeing herself as needing therapy would rob her of her last bit of self-respect.

I decided that an extended crisis intervention would be meaningful, so I asked the questions that would give me the information necessary to judge whether my idea was feasible. I asked her how she had dealt with stress in other situations.

She replied that she had never experienced stress before in her life, that until now there simply hadn't been any tensions; she seemed not to have noticed them. Thus, the eruption of emotion in her crisis could well have come forth from a basically very controlled person, who had been repressing a lot of stress and aggression. I took a very positive view of this outbreak of affect. When someone accustomed to repressing stress and avoiding conflicts starts letting loose the way she did at the beginning of our encounter, that is at least a new way of behaving, and it means that this conflict must be confronted; neither the conflict nor the crisis can be repressed any longer.

Then there was the question of other sources of help available to her during the crisis intervention. "I am no longer myself," she said. "Everyone has changed." Judging from the way she acted and spoke, all spheres of her life were involved in the crisis. Having gotten deeply into the core of her being, the disease's effects radiated outward to all aspects of her life. Next I asked her how her husband had reacted to the disease. She thought he took it very well. He visited her every day in the hospital, passed on to her all the information he had received, talked with her about the treatment methods that had been planned. He had told her what he felt about the difficulties that the disease might present for their conjugal life: nothing fundamental would change for him.

She had thus found him to be sympathetic and helpful. And yet, there was a note of skepticism: "That nothing will change—one had better not count on that. He just *says* that. He says that my scar does not bother him, but surely it *does* bother him profoundly." Their relationship, seeming on the whole capable of bearing stress, was called into question.

Asked how the children had reacted to the disease, she replied that they were actually very loving. They wanted to see the scar, but she could not allow that. She repeated the closeness/distance problem she was having with the children at the time.

This patient seemed to have relationships that were capable of bearing some of the load. There were people who could carry her through, persons who could bear with her, who could be loving with her.

I ask her about dreams. She dismissed the existence of dreams energetically.

With regard to instrumental aids, which might have become necessary at a later stage, the question arose of participation in a self-help group of affected women as a way of getting information about breast cancer and how to deal with it. Her oncologist had already made this suggestion and had met with rejection.

I presented the option of carrying out a crisis intervention together with the goal of establishing a relationship with the disease. I told her I had an impression of the disease coming over her like an avalanche. She would have to find a new way of relating to this situation, a way to take into account both death as well as survival.

I told her I imagined that the anger and hurt over her disfigured body would have to be worked through. We would have to allow for the fear of having to live with the disease no less than for the fear of dying from it. And we would be asking what meaning the disease had for her. Not of least importance would be getting her relationships with her husband and children back to normal.

I asked her to call me the next day if she wanted to go through with the crisis intervention. I intentionally used the term "crisis intervention," suggesting some twelve hours for working through the problems I had named.

"Well," she responded, "I do have a crisis, but a crisis is nothing out of the ordinary is it?"

I emphasized that it would only be out of the ordinary if she did *not* have a crisis.

The next morning she called and told me briefly that she had dreamt of me cooking in her kitchen. She would now be quite glad to accept my offer of a crisis intervention. She would like to have an hour with me in three days.

She opened this next session by telling me that she had been feeling guilty about her outburst from previous meeting. I had gone pale and she had felt sorry for me.

I put her at ease by telling her that it seemed right to me for her to let out her anger in a scream, even if it had made me go pale. She added that she had always been very envious of others, but now more than ever. She envied the health of every person she saw. But recently the possibility occurred to her that they could be in an even worse condition than she.

After bringing up the the problem of envy, she showed me the dream she had mentioned on the telephone:

> My psychotherapist is in my kitchen. At first the thought gives me a scare: Have I cleaned up? Then I realize it doesn't even matter anymore. She stands at my stove as if it happened every day, using many ingredients with

great skill. I think, who will put back all the things she has yanked out? It
smells delicious, and I am happy to have someone cooking for me.

This was the dream that followed our very stormy initial consultation, a so-called initial dream. Associating to it, she said she was very ashamed that she had screamed at "the psychotherapist" (objectifying me by referring to me in this way). She went on to say that she loved being spoiled, but that the woman in the dream made her nervous because she used so many ingredients and took everything so matter-of-factly out of the cupboards without asking. She, by contrast, is a very tidy cook and would never dare to allow such disorder.

I understood the dream as a reaction to our encounter in the crisis-intervention hour. The dream showed me several things about the dreamer: cleaning up is important for her, and everything has to be ship shape, even in a crisis. Within this framework, I, the psychotherapist, am very threatening to her since I might "yank out" too many things. This conception of hers was probably related to my having already opened up various areas of her life for discussion, which, of course, was necessary in order to determine whether I could carry out the crisis intervention. That corresponded to the "yanking out" of various drawers. Then again, she was obviously in need of motherly care, which I indeed gave her. The psychotherapy took place in a central location: the kitchen, which has to do with cooking, that is, with attending to one's body and with being taken care of. The kitchen is a very intimate place, and it is rather unusual to let someone else come in and take over. Clearly the psychotherapist should be nurturing and motherly. And yet, I should maintain an objective distance, as suggested by her speaking of me as "the psychotherapist." This distancing means I should not get too personal with her or come too close to her. On the basis of this dream, I told myself that it would be very important to be motherly with her, that she would have to find a motherly relationship to her body, and that I should not crowd her—I should really stay in the role of "the psychotherapist." Wariness of intimacy seemed to belong to this woman's personality. Also she could not allow herself to lose self-respect, and she had to keep in control—according to her standards—and live a bit frugally. She might become frightened if a relationship got too close, if all her cabinets were yanked open too boldly, revealing her secrets.

After I interpreted the dream to her in this fashion, she still repeated herself, "You know, it's simply miserable of me: at night you cook for me in a dream, which I love, and in the daytime I scream at you."

I pointed out to her that the dream in which I had been cooking came the night *after* the day in which she had screamed at me. This showed that the dream was saying I was quite capable of handling the situation. I was beginning to get the impression that she had gotten hung up on a familiar conflict in order to avoid having to talk about the threat that I really represented to her. I asked her about this and she replied that she didn't think I would frighten her in the least.

Next I went into the problem of envy, which she had brought up. Blushing, she said to me, yes, she envies me because I can live a long life, because my body is not disfigured, because I can wear a bikini, because I can still enjoy life, because I can have what I want without worrying about it, without always having to think about medications, because I can have any man I want, because I have unlimited energy, because I have nothing to fear . . . , and then she started over again from the top. These envy motifs had little to do with me as a real woman. They showed rather what sort of ideal life she envisioned for a woman, a woman whom she must have assumed was lost to her, without yet admitting this to herself. The offense of a disfigured body was mentioned. But also expressed in her envy was a longing for the joy of life, a longing which had not previously been a major concern of hers. She now projected all of this onto me.

Then we went deeper into the various aspects of her envy. When we came to the unlimited energy she ascribed to me, she suddenly had to laugh, "I envy you for something you don't have either, but I wish I had it all."

I interpreted her envy to her as a desire to recover and as a longing for an ideal of life that had not yet been fulfilled, but also as grief over the life she believed had been lost, in that order. What she envied here was an illusion; even if she did not have cancer, she would still have to leave these illusions behind one day. I tried to make her see that an illness forces us to leave certain things behind, that it was important to mourn the loss of our possibilities, that a point would come when she would have to leave illusions behind even if she hadn't had the disease. It had all just become much more urgent now.

This had quite an impact on her. She admitted how incredibly difficult it was for her to leave illusions behind. She cried a little and then pulled herself together. "But everyone has to do that," she added, having instantly become very brave again.

My remark that not everyone has to do it so radically made her think. I explained that there was a big difference between noticing in the course of one's life that certain illusions must be left behind, and being forced into it so radically by a disease.

My intention was to keep her in contact with her feelings, to cut off her determination to be brave, to blunt her tendency to take the bull by the horns before it was time. I also wanted to convey to her an appreciation for the specialness of her disease and even for the greatness it contained.

Her reaction was, "I am quite afraid I can't manage all of that."

Here the hour ended. So far, she had ended every encounter by gaining access to her anxiety and standing up to it.

In the next hour, I asked her to tell me about her life. She was the third child in a family of bureaucrats. Life at home was highly structured and everything was clean. They lived rather poorly, although money wasn't lacking. It was as if a cult had been set up around poverty. Her father put himself under enormous pressure to achieve; achievement meant everything. Dora was good, bright, never caused any problems, never asked for too much of anything. She was able to do everything very well, in contrast to her older sisters. Thus she had become the star of the family and had "a reserved seat beside her father" (her expression). She was apparently very much a father's daughter. Her mother didn't even come up in her story. Later she told me her mother was just as orderly, reliable, hard-working, and anxious as her father, but she didn't really play any role in her life.

Dora was educated to be a teacher. "And I was also a good, controlled, reliable, and hard-working teacher." She felt guilty whenever she didn't complete her work flaw-lessly. On the whole, she constantly felt guilty for thinking it was not possible to deal perfectly with children. Now, children cannot be perfectly dealt with, and whoever tries is bound to feel guilty.

She seemed to be a rather obsessive woman, the sort for whom it is important to fulfill the demands placed upon her. From her father she learned to value conscien-tiousness and control.

On the subject of relationships, she mentioned that she once had a girlfriend from school, but had lost track of her. When she was twenty, she met her husband at her first job. She felt that he knew how to live better than she did, meaning that he knew how to be a little permissive with himself and less controlled than she. In fact, he was not controlled enough so that she always had to clamp down on him. For a long time she remained single in the hope of someone better coming along. Apparently this was no secret to her future spouse. But no one better came along, and they finally married. She said she enjoys roaming through nature with him, playing sports, going into the mountains. He also likes to dance; she, however, doesn't. She is more philosophically inclined. I looked at her questioningly, and she explained that she was interested in how things cohere, how life is at all possible in the first place, what God is. She reads Kant.

I asked about any tensions there might have been between them lately. She said she was constantly afraid that her husband would one day find another, warmer woman, a woman less bent on "bringing him up." She very quietly added that he was always running up debts and that this distressed her no end.

I inquired about her sexual life, although I knew from the dream that I should not be yanking out all the drawers. Sexuality was unimportant to her, she responded, now even less important than before. For her husband, it was much more important, but they had found a good, workable compromise. "On the outside it was a good life with him," she said in a brooding tone. "But it was not alive."

She startled herself with her own statement. "This is the first time I have felt afraid and angry about the relationship and the life I've frittered away. I'm so confused." She began to complain, but managed to pull herself out of it right away. "That's right; I can't complain; if I do, I'll lose all my self-respect, and you'll lose your respect for me, too."

Evidently it did not take much for her to lose her self-respect. She lost it when she admitted to herself the feeling of having failed, perhaps when she acknowledged having any feelings at all. She projected her loss of self-respect onto me. Having her feelings breaking out was obviously quite stressful for her. She could respect herself only when she could keep her feelings under control. This is readily understandable if one recalls her life-story: she had to be orderly and controlled. But now feelings kept breaking out of her, and by stirring up these feelings yet further, I only added to her stress.

I attempted to interpret her state of mind to her: it was difficult for someone as controlled as she was to discover how many different feelings lived inside of her. It was also difficult to see suddenly that a relationship she had found quite adequate had not really given her everything she wanted. But from a therapeutic standpoint, it was very important that she allow for all these feelings. Still, I was very aware that I was causing her additional stress by encouraging her to embrace such feelings.

She responded with a promise to work on it at home. This never ceased to amaze me about Dora: she would always take careful note of everything discussed in the hour and then practice it—e.g., allowing for her feelings—at home in the presence of her family. Her family, in the meantime, was growing increasingly irritated.

I had the feeling that Dora was someone who was not really at home in her body. So I asked her what sort of relationship she had had to her body before her illness.

"A completely normal one," she answered. She asked only that her body function, and she kept it clean in return. Only very seldom did it go on strike. Here she presented an example of that notion we so often encounter according to which the body is a galley slave that must simply obey.[3] This "completely normal" relationship that she had with her body in fact amounted to the lack of a relationship. But she said that she was glad I had returned to the subject of her body. She simply could not cope with its disfiguration.

At this difficult spot I tried using the method of imagination (an imaging exercise employing fantasy) to bring her into closer contact with her body.[4] I asked her to relax and then invited her to get in touch with her body by telling me what sort of sensation she had. She felt the aching of her scar. I then asked her to visualize her body.

Responding to my directions she said, "I see myself in the city standing before a window display. I am wearing an elegant dress. No one sees anything. Everything is fine."

This was the first image she had of herself: in the city, before a display window, wearing an elegant dress; no one sees "anything," everything is fine; an attempt to nullify the loss. Dora was, by the way, a very elegant woman. The image was fitting.

For me, the key words were, "No one sees anything," so I asked her to find an image in which one could see something. Her image: "I see myself in a hospital bed. I am standing in the doorway. From there I look at the hospital bed. Everything is disgustingly white. I am under the covers, under the white covers. No one sees anything; I am covered up."

She saw herself twofold: at once in the hospital bed and at the same time looking at the bed from the doorway. Everything is disgustingly white, and again one sees nothing. For me, the key sentence was, "Everything is disgustingly white." The disgust! When I asked her about this she talked about the disgust she felt for her body, now and in general, and how she found the disease disgusting.

Suddenly she said to me, "Disgusting things are not the subject of conversation."

I looked at her, astonished, and responded, "Yes, they are; if one wants to get well, one has to talk about everything." We continued talking about disgust.

In our conversation about disgust one could clearly make out the themes of disease as failure, disease as disgusting. She was under the influence of the notion that people find those who are sick disgusting and that sick people cannot therefore be treated any more as normal human beings. All of those crudely human things take over: sweat, body odor, everything really creaturely, all of which is, of course, a reminder of ultimate death. For Dora, all of this belonged to the subject of disgust.

Suddenly she announced, "Now I want to have another image. I should be able to look at the scar in a fantasy."

It was quite remarkable how Dora had retained the obedience of her childhood, and how wonderfully her readiness to achieve worked for us now. I told her to have images, and images she had. She had mentioned that her father had put her under great pressure to achieve. Having internalized this pressure, she now drew on it to look at the scar! Everything inherited from childhood has a positive as well as a negative side!

Her image: "Now I see myself in bed. It is no longer a hospital bed. I try to push the sheet back a little. My heart is pounding like crazy!"

I realized—empathically imagining myself in her place— that she had gotten stuck. I suggested, "Why don't you try feeling the scar with your hand, without yet looking at it." I had felt the need to mitigate her pressure to achieve. "Yes, I can do that," she said, relaxing.

She touched her real scar and began to cry. "I have lost my breast before I even realized what a breast is."

I told her to make contact with her other breast.

"That's difficult; it seems somehow indecent."

"Aren't you allowed to enjoy your body?"

"I've never been allowed to enjoy my body. All of that was disgusting. But now, if I am dying, I *can* enjoy my body. I can look at my scar now, too. It hurts. It's a wound. It hurts a lot."

She cried and looked at the other breast. "I feel a bit loving toward the other breast, the healthy one. Is that all right?"

"Of course; that can only do good."

"Now I feel myself with one breast that is missing and one breast that I love. I want to cry, I want to laugh, I want to be happy, and it's completely horrible."

This was her attempt to get in touch with her disfigured body. Of course, it would have been nice if she could have found loving feelings for the scar, too, but that might have been asking too much. I restrained myself in any case.

She came to the fifth hour quite cheered up. She said that at home she had gotten in touch with her body. She had gotten in touch with each and every part, without leaving anything out. It was an incredible, fantastic experience. Now she was glad she had so much time. Now she had time for herself, too. I couldn't help but admire her for having gotten in touch with her entire body. I found it amazing that someone who for forty years had only required that her body function could, while suffering from the shock of a disease, get in touch with her body.

Apart from this news, she continued, things weren't going so well at home. Things were happening with me here in the consulting room, but at home everyone was so repressed. There was no more talk about cancer. There was no more mention of any problems at all. She was back sleeping again in the same bed with her husband. And she was back in the family routine again. Her retreat had really been a response to the crisis. But everyone was being so strangely considerate to her. Everyone was behaving as if she were no longer capable of lifting a finger, which was simply ridiculous. She would like to bring the whole family with her to see me.

First we considered what significance her wish could have for our relationship. At this point, I was still "the psychotherapist" for her. Basically we had a very friendly rapport, but always on the grounds that I represented "her psychotherapist." It had become clear to her that the entire family had to have a talk and she felt they could do that only in my presence. With the theme of envy fresh in my mind, I asked her if sharing me with the family might not make her feel jealous. She couldn't let that worry her, she responded. If she got jealous, then she would just have to be jealous.

Getting the family involved in a crisis intervention can be very important, since they are, after all, also affected by the crisis.

The family came to the sixth hour, a lively bunch. The children were very anxious to know what would happen. The husband was a bit embarrassed but nonetheless grateful.

Dora let loose right away, "You are all acting so inhibited at home. You behave so strangely, you 'infantilize' me (using a word not understood by the children). You just make me into a child, and I can't stand it. I am afraid. I want to defy you. I am angry, and I don't know what to do with you. I'm afraid that you will leave me, but I'm also afraid that I might leave you."

It all came bursting out of her. Then suddenly she got hold of herself. "My God, now I have really lost my cool." The others interrupted her with their own loss of composure. Everyone was crying and talking at the same time. It was the same with them, they said, taking each other into their arms, comforting each other. They didn't know how to treat her, they complained. They wanted so badly to do the right thing for her, but didn't know what that was.

There was a real emotional chaos. Far from being scorned for her outburst, as she had feared, she received a great deal of sympathy. Everyone assured her that they could treat her much better if she would tell them how she felt.

That was the sixth hour. They all expressed their desire to come again. They wanted to repeat the experience of feeling so wonderfully close to each other. Evidently the chaos had afforded them a rare moment of intimacy.

They came together again to the seventh hour. One sensed that the ice had been broken, and they confirmed that it was much easier for them to live together now. "Mother tells us when we mother her too much, but she also tells us when we ask too much of her. We talk with each other now."

The six-year-old girl blurted out, "We still can't look at her scar. When will you tell Mommy we want to look at her scar?"

Her mother responded that she herself had to get a little more used to the scar before she could show it to her.

Then this six-year-old girl suddenly wanted to know what would become of her when her mother died. This question received serious discussion: How did the children imagine this? How did the husband feel about it? I asked them to consider that the point was not only to think about what would happen if their mother died but also to develop ideas together about how to keep living with her. They all looked at me in amazement. It seemed that this family had really agreed that their mother would die.

The twelve-year-old son spoke of how hard it was for him. He could maybe imagine some day not having a mother any more, but when he had to imagine losing his mother at the same time as he had to imagine not losing her, it was very, very hard.

The six-year-old girl was always able to express her feelings with total clarity. "If you are dying," she said, for example, "we at least want to love you until you die. If you keep on living, that's good, too." Coming from her was something very warm and completely spontaneous.

The eldest daughter seemed very rigid and pensive. She was afraid of having to take over the role of mother. She preferred to study math!

At the end of the hour, the husband requested that he be able to come to see me one time alone with his wife. The children generously agreed.

So the couple came to the eighth hour, and soon she was accusing him: "If you weren't such a spendthrift, I wouldn't always have to control you. If you didn't always get out of line, I wouldn't always have to make you behave. And if you didn't always have everything imaginable in your head, I wouldn't always have to clamp down on you."

"Yes," he defended himself, "but when you always clamp down on me, then I have to keep coming up with something outrageous; otherwise everything gets so boring. I can't live like that, I can't breathe like that."

A classical case of collusion is presented to us: he the spendthrift, she the thrifty one; he the man who knows how to live, probably without worrying himself much about the cost, she the one who always sets the limits again by saying things like, "You can't do that; that's too much of a good thing; there you have gone too far again." He had often run up debts, and she told how she always had to find a way to pay them off. She made a lot of accusations.

I interpreted their dynamic as a couple to them along the following lines. He could only be so generous because she controlled him; she could only be so orderly because he had so much excess in store. Basically I thought this dynamic was what had kept them together. She had probably seen in him someone who could live, and he in her someone who made sure he didn't "fray too much at the edges" (his expression). It was his great fear that he would "run amok" again if his wife died because he would no longer have anyone to keep him under control. She looked at him angrily. "You'd better not think I'm going to use the last years of my life to keep you under control," she said. "That is simply out. From now on you can have that job for yourself! And what's more, from now on your debts are your problem."

He took a deep breath and declared his acceptance of her decision. He confessed that he was very afraid of being left and that this fear made him behave very oddly. Sometimes he felt the need to be close to her, while at other times he felt he needed to be separate from her because he thought he really should learn to live without her. But when he withdrew from her, she took this as a sign that he didn't love her.

This is a dynamic often encountered with couples when one of the partners is terminally ill. Both have great difficulty uniting their desire for greater closeness with their knowledge that they must part in the end. Thus they often fail to be close while they still have the chance. The only way to deal with this is to talk together and tell each other why one is withdrawing right now, for example, because one is seized again by the fear of being left alone.

This talk afforded Dora the important realization that her husband also had prob-lems with the situation. Until now, he had always passed himself off as someone who could cope with the situation without getting too upset. Sensing his anxiety and powerlessness, she could again feel close to him.

Finally the sexual issue was raised. He had told her he could live with her scar. Of course, it had been nicer before; of course, it is more beautiful when a woman has two breasts; but he could live with the scar. She took his statement as a gesture of pity. She felt that it did not represent his true feelings. He insisted that it did.

I remarked that it is often difficult to accept such a scar, not only for aesthetic reasons but also because it is a constant reminder of the disease and of possible death. However, it could also be a sign that the disease had been brought under control. This is difficult to communicate to a partner already suffering from the scar.

"I can't touch it," he responded quietly. "It reminds me of death. Still, it is true—I can live with the scar in spite of it. And I want to learn to touch it, too."

At the close of this hour, Dora announced that she wanted to come again by herself. After all, she had only four more hours. (We had agreed on twelve hours.)

In the ninth hour she seemed very depressed. Yet she said of herself, "I am now in a totally aggressive phase. You can't imagine how aggressive I am. I tell everyone I have cancer; they should all just be shocked."

"And are they actually shocked?" I asked in response.

"Yes, yes; everyone is shocked."

She repeated that cancer is a shocking disease and that you can really scare people with it. As she continued, I was getting the impression that this aggressiveness was not her predominant feeling. I commented, "I just think that it is very, very difficult for you to accept your disease,"

"Yes, it *is* difficult," she responded. "This disease got so many things moving in my life. I have never before felt so good about the family. But that's just one part of it. I still have cancer."

On account of the sheer intensity of change she had experienced, she seemed almost to have forgotten this. The feeling of being threatened had now taken hold of her again. She would probably have to become depressed again, to be confronted again with the feeling that her disease could be a disease ending in death. I interpreted her depression in this fashion, sidestepping her aggressive reaction formation. It was, of course, quite conceivable that the termination of the crisis intervention, now within sight, was also contributing to this shift of moods. For here was yet another loss looming up.

But we should not forget that the theme of disgust associated with the disease was no longer being addressed, despite its great importance.

She came to the tenth hour and said she really didn't want to exceed the twelve hour limit, but would nevertheless like to see me every now and then in the future to talk about any other problems that might come up. Would that be possible?

We agreed that we would work together for two more hours, and that subsequently she should come to see me whenever she felt the need to discuss a problem. (Up until this point, we had worked for one and a half hours twice a week for the first two weeks of the crisis intervention, then once a week during the eight following weeks.)

She enumerated in this hour what we had and had not accomplished in relation to the goals that we had formulated in the first hour. Now she felt it was imperative for her to know what the disease meant for her, and this was how she wanted to use our time. "It just can't be a mistake when one gets cancer," she said. By this she meant that there must be sufficient reason for it. "I have tried hard to do everything right my whole life, and now I have cancer. But my sister, who never gave the slightest thought about how to live life correctly, always gives in to her inclinations, and never worries about duty, is as healthy as can be."

The notion that one doesn't get sick if one lives correctly was next to holy writ for her. Living correctly had meant living according to an ethic of duty. Now she was beginning to ask herself if this giving into one's inclinations—as her sister had done without a second thought—might not be legitimate after all. She was no longer so sure she knew what it meant to live "correctly."

However, she still couldn't seem to free herself of the thought that in spite of her efforts to live correctly, she was nevertheless punished with a disease. Punishment for what? She began searching for situations in her life in which she behaved in a blameworthy manner. She magnified these situations, spoke of guilt feelings she ought to have had but did not actually experience. I offered the interpretation that attitudes which had previously been vital to her were no longer salutary for her life. Looked at it in this way, the disease would not only be a hint, but also a chance, for her to change.

We approached the question of guilt and possible punishment in a gentler fashion by asking ourselves what the disease had changed in her life. She felt that the disease had changed her and that the change had been total, for all but the rudiments of her restraint had disappeared. Now she knew that control is not everything. She sensed that she was much more alive when she expressed her feelings, and she was happy knowing that she could have feelings. The prospect of death had rendered meaningless any masking of her feelings. She could now express her feelings and needs honestly, even when they were fairly childish. This was only possible, she believed, in the face of her impending death. She felt that she had become much more honest, spontaneous, and warm. This had done wonders for her.

By having her say what had changed in her life, I was indirectly trying to show her what she still owed to the disease, what she could now integrate into her life thanks to the disease. She found this illuminating, but she kept returning to the thought that she must have done much more in her life that was wrong. Finally, we agreed that we are always doing things wrong in life and that such a disease demonstrates to us precisely that life cannot be lived perfectly. Besides, I told her, it could be dangerously false to believe that disease is a punishment. One hardly thinks of health as a special reward.

These discussions, which characterized the twelfth hour as well, wearied me. I tried to direct her attention to the future, asking her to think more about how she wanted to deal with herself, her disease, and her life, than about everything that might have been wrong. I tried to interpret the disease to her as an existential crisis to which she had surrendered, through which new perspectives had come into her life. Feeling warmer and more alive was not a bad outcome after all.

In the last hour she wanted to know what I thought about life after death. First, I asked to hear her fantasy.

For her, dying meant gaining peace from the demands of others. That was the most important part of it to her; it is something one often hears from cancer patients. Apparently they are persons who easily allow themselves to be overburdened by the demands of the environment, probably not so much because the environment is so demanding, but rather because they experience its demands so compellingly, as demands that they must fulfill in order to be loved.

I asked her if she really found it necessary to die right away just to gain peace from the demands of others. Couldn't she accomplish this in some other way?

She laughed.

We spoke about the many different ways of conceiving of death and the world to come. We exchanged our different fantasies of the other world. I suggested she read the book Blick nach drueben [Glimpse of the Other Side] by Wiesenhuetter.[5] Wiesenhuetter had a thrombosis of the lung and lay in a coma for an extended period of time, after which he wrote in a sober style about what he had experienced.

As we spoke about dying, it became clear that she interpreted death as failure. Disease had meant failure to her, and now dying did as well. And yet, she had only said aloud what we all probably feel inwardly from time to time: "One should not die, and if one does, then this is a failure."

"If it is a failure," I responded, "it is a failure we all have in common, a sign that failure belongs generally to life." Again we talked about how difficult it was for her to fail and about how she must really learn to fail.

That was the last hour of the crisis intervention proper. She came again four weeks later to talk, addressing me for the first time by name. She had never used my name during the crisis intervention. Only now could she begin to have a personal relationship with me. The remaining meetings over the next two years consisted of talks at intervals of six to eight weeks. She usually brought a dream that she wanted to discuss. The main theme was Dora as a skillful, self-confident, sensible woman, one side of whom was a helpless child. The child in her, unloved, had given up. Going along with this was the theme of learning to be motherly with herself. She had me assuring her that she not only *could* be but also must be motherly with herself. More and more I became for her someone whose perspectives allowed her to test and call into question demands that she had taken over from her father. There was also the matter of learning to see that her sister, whom she despised and whom she related to me from time to time, was the one who lived out her own shadow sides. Dora had these other qualities, too, which she came slowly to recognize as belonging to herself.

At present, we continue to see each other approximately every six months. Dora has gone now for some six years without a relapse. She is looking good, pursues her work, and has changed a lot.

This crisis intervention shows how in a crisis of loss, although one's entire life is currently dominated by the loss, the depth of the crisis reveals itself to the affected person only with time.

When the crisis is admitted, changes in experience and behavior come to pass. In the face of a fundamental crisis, parts of a person previously held in check can be allowed to live to an extent otherwise hardly imaginable. Incidentally, in her mourning work, one could often see Dora repeating the second phase of chaotic emotions and the transition into the third phase. This is typical in crises of loss; it shows that new aspects of life continue to get caught up in the crisis, and that new insights and new experiences continue to issue forth from it. In addition, one can see that Dora did not actually make her farewell. She did not actually have to take leave from life or from her children. Among other factors, this had to do with the fact that the crisis intervention took place during an early phase of her illness, when she did not yet feel any loss of physical strength.

This crisis intervention also shows how a variety of supremely important problems are only mentioned and touched on in this process, and yet how changes can and do take place. Dora went through an individuation process. She detached herself—as was quite essential at her age—from the values represented by her father. She began asking herself which values she regarded as conducive to her life. In this regard she became more motherly to herself. She found what was for her a good balance between emotional life and experience, and the need to be in control.

Intervention vs. Short-Term Therapy

This case example affords us a good opportunity to compare crisis intervention and short-term therapy. While crisis interventions are initiated in response to urgent crises, they are often carried out in the style of a short-term therapy, as in the foregoing example.

Short-term therapy denotes a form of therapy that employs depth-psychological theory and technique in a way that requires fewer meetings, arranged in a less formal sequence, than does full-term analysis. Short-term therapies can, however, extend over a long period of time.[6]

Short-term therapy differs importantly from crisis intervention in the following respect: the beginning of a crisis intervention is marked by a concentrated succession of meetings, and only later, when a more thorough treatment of the most pressing problems is called for, is a less formal sequence of meetings offered.

An attempt is made in both procedures to resolve a circumscribed problem or set of problems by guiding those persons seeking therapy to perceive their feelings and needs and to find strategies for coping with their problems. Malan, the founder of psychoanalytic short-term therapy, named the following indications for short-term therapy: a mild psychopathology; good ego-strength, that is, an ego showing evidence of having mastered all the major transitions in life without the development of symptoms, at least without the development of chronic symptoms; good motivation for treatment; and an understandable, circumscribed problem whose resolution is imperative.[7]

These criteria, now out of date, continue to be applied as an ideal to candidates for short-term therapy, and even to those in need of a crisis intervention. An ideal client for crisis intervention would be someone with good ego-strength who is normally healthy and is now confronted with a problem appearing for the first time. It should already have become clear that this model client hardly exists, not to mention the fact that crisis interventions must be made precisely when an individual is in the middle of a crisis, at which time ego-strength is rather difficult to estimate.

Today, ego-strength is no longer a prerequisite either for crisis intervention or for short-term therapy. Rather, therapists engaged in such procedures are often called upon to lend their own ego-function to their clients until they are once again capable of drawing on their own.[8] For example, we say, "If I put myself in your place, I feel. . . ." But today's method of short-term therapy still requires that the problem at hand be understandable, and crisis intervention still requires a discernible primary problem which is not identical to the conflict that precipitated the crisis. Moreover, the anxiety triggered by the crisis must, within limits, be tolerable to the therapist as well as to the person in crisis. In addition, it is crucial in both processes for a relationship to be established without delay. In crisis intervention, the signal is given that a relationship has taken shape when the person in crisis relaxes.

The therapist proceeds actively with both methods. Transference events are interpreted immediately. Apart from a different organization of appointments, the difference between crisis intervention and short-term therapy consists of candidates for short-term therapy having sufficient motivation to confront themselves with their problems. For individuals in crises, the crisis which has them in its grips is motivation enough. The crisis takes the place of motivation.

In addition, the events of a crisis usually have an existential ripple effect on related persons, who in most cases must also be involved in the therapeutic conversation, if one wishes to avoid handing the crisis on from one person to another.

Chapter 7

Couples in Escalating Conflict

A married couple, he 33, she 28, came to me for therapy. Married for six years, they had been having frequent fights for as long as they had known each other. They reported that earlier they had simply shouted at each other. Lately, however, they had been getting into heavy, violent confrontations. The situation was steadily degenerating. In their fights, they goaded each other into ever greater acts: if she hit him with a shoe, he would grab the kitchen chair, and she would come back with a needle to stick him. Beside themselves with rage, they would both lose control. A friend who lived downstairs and heard the noise usually came up and threatened to call the police. This made them furious and they would curse him; then they felt better. The friend had suggested to them that they receive marriage counseling. They themselves would not have thought of it, but they admitted that their friend was right: their condition could not be tolerated. A change was urgently needed.

I asked them what they conceived the goal of marital therapy to be. They said they wanted to learn to fight less, to understand each other better, or else, she added, to separate. He did not react to this suggestion of hers. While he saw their main problem as the inability of either of them to give in, she saw it as his inability to accept the fact that she made more money than he did. To get even, he would put her down. Immediately he countered, "But you always put me down, too."

"That didn't seem to occur to you before," she responded.

"Of course that occurred to me," he answered back. "I just didn't say it."

"You aren't even capable of coming up with a thought of your own."

"And you have always had a lousy character. Luckily, that is showing up here right away."

They continued fighting in this manner without any substantially new accusations being made.

I listened to the verbal exchange, amazed at its rapidity. I felt bad about how they hurt each other. But I sensed that neither of them was the least bit able to let himself or herself really feel hurt. Back and forth it passed in front of me like an exchange of volleys. Feeling more and more like a spectator and an audience, I finally interrupted them to inform them that I had heard enough; they had demonstrated their problem very convincingly to me. I could easily imagine that they could keep this fighting up for hours to come.

"Yes, but at some point one of us blows a fuse," he said. "Then we get violent. That's not so nice."

Both nodded guiltily.

I asked them how it was after the fight. First, they each either retreated or went out. A few hours later, they met in the kitchen, where each would prepare a separate meal. In the end they would make up again. For a while, things were good between them, but before long, two days at most, they would start fighting again, in spite of having resolved not to.

I asked how a reconciliation could take place at all if neither of them was willing to give in.

She informed me, "There is a sentence that one of us always says, which goes, 'We better clean up our act, or else they will see the mess we are in.' " "They" referred to friends who might appear. It was very important to them to keep their fighting a secret. Those friends who knew of it were repeatedly called in for help, but the others didn't know about it. "We need people to come between us. Sometimes I think we could kill each other," were his exact words.

"That I doubt," she said. "We watch out for each other."

I asked them if there was a typical situation that precipitated their quarrels. It was always petty things, they unanimously replied, with each wanting to stay in the right. She could say something as simple as, "The weather is really nice." He might answer that it could be nicer. "No, it is nice . . . ," etc. And so the fight would escalate. All that counted from then on was staying in the right.

But it could hardly have been as simple as they had depicted it. This one example alone gives rise to the suspicion—still to be tested—that she was more satisfied with her life than he and that he could not bear that. Perhaps he had the more depressive disposition of the two. But let us leave this matter for now and continue on with the case. Since my impression was that they were beyond the point of being able to listen to each other, I asked them what accusations they had heard in their fight at the beginning of the session.

"She says I am stupid and unfit for life," he reported. "The only way I can defend myself is with violence."

"No, I didn't say that," she contended.

I interrupted them and asked her if she would kindly tell me what accusations she had heard.

"Yes, but I do have to justify myself," she insisted.

"I can well understand your need to justify yourself," I responded. "This 'having to justify oneself' surely plays a huge role in your fights. You can justify yourself afterward if you like, but first I would like to know what accusations you have heard."

"Yes, that is true about the justifications," she affirmed. "I heard that I have a lousy character, I am a nasty women's libber, I never give in."

"But I didn't say that this time. . . ."

I cut him off to remark, "Both of you seem to have heard things no one said."

We rewound the tape and listened to the fight word for word. Their reactions:

"You said neither one of us can give in!" she noted.

"You don't say I'm dumb and unfit for life," he observed, "but that I cannot accept the fact that you make more money than I. And you didn't say violent either. How could I have misheard so many things?"

He looked at me questioningly. "Maybe you are afraid of your wife thinking you are dumb, unfit, and violent," I suggested.

I intentionally intimated a projection without insisting on it. That way he could decide himself if he wanted to deal with these traits as belonging to him, which put him under less pressure.

"I am like that sometimes," he said, "but only as a reaction to her when she. . . ."

"And now you would like to justify yourself?" I queried.

He laughed and signaled with his hand that he was giving the floor to his wife.

"I also completely forgot about the put down. That's important. But about the lousy character," she announced triumphantly, "that I have not forgotten."

"The charge of being a women's libber came out of thin air?" I asked.

"That comes from other fights," he answered in an equally triumphant tone.

I instructed them both to listen very carefully in their coming fights for what was actually said, for what forms of put-down were used, and for how the self-justifications operated.

Many couples can be brought by means of such instructions to fight more consciously. Escalation can then be held within bounds. This was not yet the actual crisis intervention, which was still to come, but an excerpt from an initial consultation.

This initial conversation clearly demonstrates a couple falling into a symmetrically competitive power-collusion, which is in the process of escalating.[1] This means that they both had a problem with power and powerlessness in the relationship, and that they both attempted to resolve the problem while staying in the position of power. We speak of escalation in this respect when both parties exercise power and control over each other in an exchange that can only increase in force and intensity.

This leads to the conclusion that this couple's relationship was being strained by some additional factor. It could have been a more external form of stress: increased alcohol consumption, for example, or employment difficulties. Or it could have been a more psychological stress, for example, the question of separation coming closer to home than ever before.

Each one attempts to defeat the other in this collusion, or at least to avoid being defeated. The mutuality and reciprocity of the winner role characterizes a symmetrical, as opposed to a complementary, power-collusion. In a complementary power-collusion, one partner always wins and the other always loses. The problem there is not so much fights that get out of hand as it is a division of roles that guarantees the same person the loser role every time. With a symmetrical arrangement of power, on the other hand, fights can work themselves up to a high pitch, as the couple in our example vividly demonstrated. At the slightest hint of powerlessness, the opponent's attack is answered with a demonstration of power, often consisting of a disparagement of the partner. The places where the most hurt can be inflicted are mutually known through repeated trial and error. Hence the term "power-collusion," meaning a mutual entanglement out of which the reaction of the one can be predicted with certainty on the basis of the reaction of the other. *Colludere* means literally "playing together." Here, however, "play" is compulsive. In an escalating power-collusion, where each tries to outdo the other, feelings of powerlessness are feared and defended against. To feel powerless means to be helpless, to be tortured, even under certain conditions to be destroyed. Power on the other hand signifies calling the shots, even being the torturer. With couples that live out a symmetrical power-collusion, both partners wage a heroic battle against becoming helpless and dependent on the other, against being tortured, without ever letting down their guards. The pattern that plays itself out in the relationship is at least a latent, if not also an acute, intrapsychic conflict. The only way feelings of helplessness and powerlessness can be kept at a distance from consciousness is with large investments of energy. Such persons are engaged in huge battles.

A symmetrical relationship of power constellates itself in a couple when both have the same fundamental problem, are frightened by the same emotions, and defend themselves against the same weaknesses. While they wage a violent battle against their partners' weaknesses, they are also battling the same weaknesses in themselves. This fighting, however, runs the risk of awakening new fears. Injuries are begrudged, fear of being abandoned grows large, and the battle must escalate further. Perhaps this collusion is so often encountered because so many persons have never learned any other form of relationship apart from that based on power. They have learned that one person is on top and the other is on the bottom, and they have made up their minds to be on top whenever possible. In our case, both had made this decision.

The power-collusion affords a defensive barrier against feelings of powerlessness and anxiety, above all against the fear of separation, but also against the need to be accepted. It also helps keep certain parts of oneself at a safe distance: one sees them and denounces them in the partner, for it would be quite disagreeable if they existed within oneself. This is related to the problem of having to defend oneself. Compulsive self-justification seduces us into a circular battle for power. When we justify ourselves, we declare ourselves to be the accused party who is seeking justice. A circle is drawn up with assignments of guilt on one side and proofs of innocence on the other. The power play is in full swing. One may rationalize this compulsive circle of self-justification by insisting that one must defend oneself "to the last," must defend against uncalled-for attacks; one has to do it for the sake of one's self-respect. But this rarely leads to a real feeling of autonomy, which was actually the point of the defense in the first place. It is much more likely to lead to a violent confrontation, to new injuries and new insults.

There are other questions more important than that of who is right. More important than self-justification is the question of feeling wounded and insulted, and whether one is getting what one feels—rightly or wrongly—entitled to. By formulating such questions, we break the vicious circle. The reason for the fight, especially an escalating one, was to defend oneself against feelings of vulnerability and insecurity. These questions allow for such feelings, which is why the asking of them is not so easily tolerated. They can even give rise to intense anxiety, which must be forcefully kept under control.

There is a popular exit from this circular power-collusion, which can at times relieve the relationship of some stress: temporary delegation of the problem to a third party. Delegation is at once both a social defense mechanism and a coping device. We are familiar with the phenomenon from daily life: two people talking together complain about a common enemy, thereby avoiding a necessary confrontation with each other. Instead of a having a confrontation, they come away feeling close to each other, as if they have an understanding. Actually they are postponing the conflict. "There's nothing wrong with us; it's the others that are no good," is the formula; a scapegoat is found to ease the tension of the situation. A relief delegation sometimes affords the quarreling couple a day or two of peace.

This defense mechanism can also be employed in crisis interventions to achieve temporary—but only temporary—relief. The couple in our example demonstrated their familiarity with this tactic when they mentioned their helpful friend who came around to intervene in case of big trouble. Afterwards they tore him apart, and that gave them relief.

Let us continue with the example. The man telephoned me the day after our initial talk. He was very agitated. He said he had really gone overboard and so had his wife. It hadn't been this bad for a long time, and the friend was not around. They were in a real fix. Might they be able to come before the appointed hour, today if possible?

I had several conflicting feelings during this telephone call. They had been fighting since the previous evening, and she already had a cut on her eyebrow. I had heard in the initial talk that the friend always had to separate the two squabblers; since the friend had resigned his post, the question was whether I should now take it over. The sentence, "We need persons to come between us," ran through my mind.

In addition, I was on a tight schedule, and an emergency meeting would have been inconvenient for me. On the other hand, he had called me during the telephone hours that I had specified. This spoke against the hypothesis that he was merely calling to ventilate at the drop of a hat. And there was considerable worry in his voice. I asked myself if I would be letting myself be used or if this really was a crisis requiring intervention.

I ran our initial talk back through my mind. I thought about what might have triggered their crisis aside from the realization that they definitely stood in need of counseling. It suddenly occurred to me that she had mentioned the possibility of a separation, and that he had showed no response whatsoever. It was as if they had agreed on the goals of their therapy, and although separation had emerged as one possible goal, it was naturally not a desirable one. In that case, he would not have been ready in the first talk to confront himself with the problem of separation. I recalled that I had not come back to it, although he had reacted so stoically.

I made up my mind and gave him a provisional appointment after my normal working hours. I suggested that they go their separate ways until that time. He informed me that they would have done that anyway since they both worked. He breathed a sigh of relief over the telephone, and I had the feeling I wasn't making a huge mistake in seeing them. However, I continued to ask myself if this crisis intervention was really a good idea. On the one hand, I thought that they should see for themselves what they had gotten themselves into; I would not be simply another mediator. But the feeling persisted that it was indeed important for them to come today. I felt concerned for them, but I also had the need to distance myself from the entire matter.

This conflict of feelings is a typical response to the question of crisis intervention within therapy. But I also believe that these conflicting feelings reflected the psychological dynamic that was operating within this couple's relationship. They both showed great concern for each other at the same time as they demonstrated the need for distance from each other.

They were both extremely tense and fidgety when they arrived in the evening. They apologized for having come before the originally appointed time, but they had not been able to think of any other way. For a moment I felt frightened by them both and concluded from this that they themselves must have been very frightened, since they posed no real danger to me. But I decided not to mention the anxiety yet.

I asked them each to outline briefly the conflict in words that gave rise to the present tension and crisis. They should try to describe the conflict and the feelings and fears associated with it.

"We were talking on the way home about what we should do next," he began. "We were in a good mood, if a bit absorbed in our thoughts. Then we realized how often we deprecate each other. I have said to my wife any number of times that she drives like an idiot."

"You yourself also drive?" I asked.

"At the moment my driver's license is suspended because of alcohol." He continued without pause, "When we arrived home, I told her I might have to look for a new job. The company is running out of contracts. I thought I was handling the situation in a responsible way. Until now there haven't been any problems with the company, but if you see something like this coming, you can still get on the ball. She immediately threw a fit, foamed at the mouth, told me I was a good-for-nothing, lazy dog. I could have let this cat out of the bag in one of our therapy sessions. So I felt I had been treated completely unfairly. I had to defend myself. I only wanted to talk it over with her. And when I defended myself, she told me that my imagination had always been the best thing about me. She said if it kept on going like this, she would get a divorce. Then I let loose on her and grabbed her really hard. I told her she would die before divorcing me. I feel really awful. I hate it when I get so violent. I really do want to be able to live with her. It's just that I'm afraid she'll leave me."

As he spoke these last two sentences, his wife's face brightened up and beamed at him for an instant, then went blank again.

She began her version, "We were very sad when we left here yesterday. We were sad that we always put each other down. We realized on the way home that we put each other down even without fighting. Then he told me the bit about his job. A little light went on in my head: whenever he has professional problems he drinks more, and then we have more fights. I saw us heading for bad times. I threw it in his face: I called him a good-for-nothing, a loafer, a lazy dog, and other such names. It wasn't very nice. And then when he started to defend himself, it sounded like he was mocking me, so I came around again with the divorce. I know that word pushes a button with him. And I feel miserable now, low down, for letting my bad experiences with him keep me from believing that he could mean it differently. And I don't really have any idea if I'm the least bit important to him. When he was talking just now, I felt that I meant something to him and I felt better."

Now he gave her a very pleased look.

This description of the precipitating situation brought into focus still other problems: his difficulties on the job and with alcohol. But it still seemed to me that the heart of the conflict was that she was very quick to propose divorce although she knew that wounded him deeply. My suspicion seemed to be confirmed: the remark she threw out during our initial talk—"or even separation"—did indeed have a delayed effect that contributed to the new conflict.

I pointed out to both of them that the possibility of divorce had already been mentioned here in the hour, perhaps not as a desirable goal of the therapy, but nevertheless as a possible one. In retrospect, it made me wonder even more why he didn't react when the thought obviously scared him so much.

As if completely taken by surprise, he said he hadn't heard it. Now even if he really wasn't conscious of having heard the remark, unconsciously, it could still have been the source of stress. I proposed that we talk about what each of them thought and felt about the prospect of divorce.

"The divorce threat always comes from me," she began. "I threaten you with divorce because you leave me too much in the dark about your feelings for me. You have always done that. When you get so desperately mad, I realize that it would kill you if I left. That reassures me that you won't go."

"But you could make it much easier on yourself," he countered. "The reason I can't ever get clear about my feelings is because you are always telling me you're going to leave me. If I'd admit to myself that you are the most important woman in my life, the most important *person* in my life, then your threats would really do me in."

I summarized: she threatens with separation, knowing that he is going to hold her back with all his might—in the crudest sense. What she was actually saying was: I am going; hold me back, tell me how much I mean to you and that you need me. He did hold her back, but he did not express his feelings for her in a positive way. Thus the game had to start over again from the beginning.

In response he said he always thought it was only he who was dependent on her, and since a man should not be dependent, he always had to put her down and could never tell her that he needed her. If she needed him, too, then he would have no problem telling her how much he needs her. At this point, both seemed to let a lot of tension go.

It was noticeable that he wanted to express his feelings and had the confidence that he could, but only when it became clear that she was as dependent on him as he was on her. The power-collusion thus remained very much in effect, which is to be expected.

She was surprised to see how ambiguous were her messages to him. She thought of herself as having a straightforward personality. And it also surprised her to realize how much she wanted him to hold her back, how intensely she provoked him to these violent tantrums. She shook her head, "How absurd to wound someone just to force a proof of love out of them!"

I asked them each if they had ever experienced anything earlier in their lives that would correspond to these feelings and this behavior in regard to separation.

He told how his mother ran away countless times. She would return after some days or weeks. Whenever she announced her departure, his father shrugged his shoulders and replied, "Go ahead; run away. See what I care." He confessed that he wanted to have a different kind of wife, someone who wasn't always thinking about running away. He had imagined a relationship in which the prospect of separation and divorce would never present itself. Every time his wife mentioned divorce, she broke an important rule of his, a rule of which she had no idea, until now. This doubled the impact of her attack and the depths to which he was shaken.

Then she told how her husband was like her father. She had never really known if she meant anything to her father. He either fantastically idolized her or else paid absolutely no attention to her, without her ever knowing what she had done wrong. Out of revenge, she abandoned him in her heart. Then he really had to work hard to win her over again. They both began to laugh.

She started to see that she dealt with her husband the same way she used to deal with her father. They talked about their childhood experiences and joined together in cursing their parents.

By asking them about their life stories, I not only opened up a way to understand their situation and behavior, but also gave them the opportunity to find solidarity with each other. Now they could see that their problem involved their parents as well.

Their weaknesses could be condemned as stemming from their parents. They had both learned something from their parents that proved harmful to life. This insight provided momentary relief for both of them. Of course, the relief was gained by delegating the problem. But to me they seemed strong enough to take this problem back out of delegation, to assume responsibility for it again in their relationship. I confirmed how disappointing it was to discover that one's partner could not after all fulfill the wishes that one's childhood experiences had made so important.

"Or when you see that the way you deal with your partner rules out the fulfillment of those wishes," she added.

"I guess that is a problem with me," he confessed. "I don't let my wife out of my sight. It's not that I react exactly the way my father did; I do just the opposite, but just as severely."

"And that infuriates me," she responded. "You are always on my back, always controlling me. I never get what I want from you."

"Well, what *do* you want?"

"Man! Do I have to say it again already? I want you to tell me clearly how you feel about me for once."

One can see that, by fighting, the greatest possible closeness could be experienced with simultaneous distance. Closeness without distance was probably still quite threatening for them, endangering each one's autonomy and sense of self.

I explained that I didn't expect them to stop fighting all of a sudden. It could be that fighting was something of a sport for them. They could introduce rules to regulate what kinds of blows were and were not allowed. But they could also start paying attention to what kinds of fears they were covering over with their fighting. Was it fear of dependence, separation, abandonment, or the loss of self-respect? In the process they might even manage to voice their fears instead of putting each other down. Then I told them I had experienced intense anxiety when they first arrived, and I asked them to tell me how they had felt at the time.

"I only felt angry and contemptuous, not afraid," she replied.

And he: "I was terrified, which is why I had to see you right away. By the way, something else occurs to me. Whenever my mother came back, my father would just sit there and sulk. Then either the pastor or the teacher had to come to sort things out. Afterward my parents would join together in tearing the mediator to pieces."

"Those are nice prospects," I comment.

They both said in response that it was exactly the same story with them. The friend had to mediate and then they tore him apart after he had left.

"And now I am taking the place of your friend? Afterward you will be tearing me apart?"

I brought this problem into the discussion intentionally. It had already been on my mind at the very beginning of our telephone conversation. I felt the danger of putting new wine in old wineskins.

They looked at each other quite shaken.

The question that I asked them to ponder was whether they would assume responsibility for their own quarrels, which could be expected to continue for now. I personally did not see it as worthwhile to step into the shoes of their friend. However, if necessary, they could count on one crisis intervention per month with me in addition to the normal therapy sessions.

As it turned out, they did not require any further intervention.

Couples engaged in escalating fighting lead one at times to think that a crisis intervention or therapy must establish harmony. They long for harmony and hope to achieve it by fighting, although this naturally never comes about. In the end, they are also afraid of harmony, which exposes them to the threat of losing their individual selfhood.

If fighting gives them peace, such couples can find happiness with each other. But it would be illusory to think that fighting is not part of the way they are. A fight can be prevented from escalating if each partner gradually learns to own up to his or her weaknesses, to the need to be taken care of, and to be dependent. Taking responsibility for one's shadow and for one's fear of one's shadow would be taking a considerable step forward.

Chapter 8

Crises in the Psychotherapeutic Process

Crises can also occur within the psychotherapeutic process, and thus so can crisis interventions.

The comparison of crisis intervention and short-term therapy in Chapter Six showed that the motivation required for a self-confrontation is provided automatically in a crisis, while it is demanded but not assumed in short-term therapy. A crisis can take the place of this so-called conscious motivation; it can be viewed as unconcious motivation, an unconscious impulse toward change.

That a crisis can replace a lacking or insufficiently conscious motivation becomes clear, at the very latest, when we therapists find ourselves wishing a crisis on an individual so that something can "get moving" psychically. There have been occasions where we have wished for this urgent compression of life that paves the way for change. The fact that a crisis can replace motivation—where crisis is understood as the expression of unconscious motivation—shows that we are proceeding from a particular conception of human beings as creatures that must bring what is inherent in themselves to a creative unfolding. They must become themselves, whether this happens at conscious or less than conscious turning points in life, which may be manifested as crises.

Defense-Centered/Conflict-Centered Work

Depth-psychologically oriented therapies deal with the confrontation of consciousness by the unconscious. The goal is the integration of unconscious impulses, ideas, fantasies, etc., into consciousness. One can explicate this according to the viewpoints of various schools. Depth-psychology in general speaks of defense, coping, and compensation mechanisms, whose purpose is to hold affects, fantasies, and drive impulses in check. In Jungian terms, one speaks of the ego-complex with its ordering, defense, coping, and compensation functions as over and against the unconscious complexes.[1] This ego-complex can be well or poorly structured, that is, more or less autonomous in relation to the parental complexes, depending on age. Therapy has to do with the interplay between the unconscious complexes and the ego-complex.

As a rule, these unconscious complexes are projected. They can be directly experienced in the analytic situation by being mirrored in the therapeutic relationship. Or they can be projected onto a life situation and become "food for thought." They can be experienced in an imaginative journey, in a fantasy, or simply in dreams. Given this psychodynamic, dialectical activity, one can work according to either a defense-centered or a conflict-centered model. Defense-centered work entails constantly supporting the ego-complex with its capacities for defense, for coping, or for compensation. Conflict-centered work implies a focus on the emotions, fantasies, and drives that are held in check by means of defenses.

Whether one will work with an emphasis on primarily conflict or defense depends in part on the diagnosis. A less well structured ego-complex will call for a more defense-centered approach; the better-structured ego-complex for a more conflict-centered approach. However, the decision to adopt one or the other approach depends not only on the diagnosis, but also on the countertransference. The more irritated the therapist, the more likely it is that he or she will work in a conflict-centered way. Here a countertransference that is not entirely determined by the actual situation also plays a role. Insecure analysands, for example, may behave arrogantly to compensate for their insecurity. If analysts do not see through this arrogance, they can end up working in a conflict-centered way. As a result, their analysands strengthen their defenses and compensations yet further, making therapy impossible.

Crisis intervention and short-term therapy follow the rule—a rule which has been my point of departure in this book—that the coping mechanisms of the person in crisis are to be addressed first. Thus only when the ego-complex has been strengthened does one then deal with the various unconscious complexes forcing their way to the surface, the emotions, the drives, the shadow, etc.

Of course, in therapies of longer duration one never works according to an exclusively defense-centered or conflict-centered model. Each perspective relieves the other and crosses over into the other. At the same time, diagnosis, countertransference, and habitual attitudes play important roles. If one is using a conflict-centered method and senses that an emotion has already passed the critical point of optimal efficacy, it is time to strengthen the defenses.

In the following case example, a forty-six-year-old man dreamt:

> I am standing among other people in a party tent. A guy my age, wearing an open shirt and a golden chain around his neck, his hairy chest on display, speaks in such a way that no one can help but listen. A young girl, age thirteen or fourteen, appears, takes an interest in him. He grabs her, presses her up close to him, and kisses her on the mouth. I had already been feeling itchy the whole time, and now I can't stand it anymore. I go up to him and tell him he is rotten bastard to puff himself up like that and rape that girl. My anger wakes me up.

This is a classic shadow dream from a man who had at the time been in analysis for about six months. He himself was very thin and blond, and had trouble coming to terms with his lack of a hairy chest. Among other things, the dream portrayed his shadow, which he both longed for and defended himself against. The hairy chest of the man in the dream, not only on display but even ornamented with a golden chain, was evidently a highly prized attribute of masculinity for him.

Every dream can be interpreted from either a defense-centered or conflict-centered perspective. If one asks dreamers to supply associations to their dreams, they unconsciously choose the approach best suited to them.

To the question, "What occurs to you in relation to this dream?" the dreamer could, for example, answer, "I told that guy off but good. I'm proud I dared to come out against him in front of everybody at the party." This would be a defense-centered perspective: he tells how he deals with the shadow figure, but says nothing about the fact that this man is someone who obviously annoys and infuriates him. Approaching the dream in a conflict-centered way, he might answer, "He is a miserable jerk, so conceited and horny." Here he would boldly go with the indignation that came out in the dream.

The sooner he allowed it to boil over, the sooner he would be asking himself—if the therapist wasn't asking him—when does *he* behave like this conceited guy (interpretation on the subjective level). This would be the conflict-centered approach. With the defense-centered approach, we would collect associations to this "shadow guy," but these associations would be allowed to remain a projection for the present. If the analysand spoke at length about where he meets men of this type, how ridiculously they behave, what kind of cars they drive, etc., and then got worked up over them, one would simply take note of it all. One would just allow for the fact that this shadow figure of his psyche was projected onto other men, remaining delegated. Only much later might the dreamer be asked what this guy was doing in his dream. One might even refrain from this question altogether.

Everything that happens in the therapeutic situation, especially interpretation of materials such as those above, can be treated in a more defense-centered or more conflict-centered way. The perspective one chooses depends not only on the perspective presented by the analysand, nor does it depend solely on the role in which the therapist sees himself or herself. It depends as well on the following theoretical consideration: to what extent is the ego-complex of the affected individual in a position to integrate the emotions released in the therapeutic process? Change in the therapeutic process cannot happen without emotions being released. Yet it is not desirable for the emotions to go overboard; just enough emotion should be released to put the ego in distress, without being more than the ego can integrate into the ego-complex or self-image. In order for the necessary changes to take place, analysis must be carried out under the steady pressure of a mild crisis.

Using Jungian psychological terminology, we speak of unconscious complexes becoming activated and integrated into consciousness. In this way, new images become accessible to consciousness, which can lead to the experience of an influx of energy. This comes about in practice when we talk about the expressive medium in which the unconscious complex manifests itself, be it a dream, a fantasy, a fear, an idea, a bodily symptom, etc.; in other words, one gives expression to the symbol. This is usually accompanied by uncomfortable, frightening, or even frighteningly euphoric feelings against which the patient begins defending. Because the patient is contained in a relationship with a therapist, and so has the security of being able to tackle the problem together with a competent helper, more material can be allowed to surface than if the patient were alone. Gradual change can thus take place.

Coming back again and again to the question of what it is that brings about change in therapy, Franck came to the conclusion that it is desirable to fan the flames of emotion until a peak that has the proportions of a crisis is reached—which can happen very early on.[2] At this peak, the analysand is in a labile phase, during which old patterns of behavior can be eradicated and an openness to new patterns can be established.

This sounds like behavioral therapy, and indeed, in this respect, there are similarities between behavioral therapy, the analytical therapy of C. G. Jung, and psychoanalysis. The similarity to Jung's theory of complexes is especially strong. What they all have in common is the idea that an effective therapy depends on emotions being stirred up to a peak of crisis proportions which is capable of changing fixed structures. These changes are not, however, to be seen as sudden and grand but rather as gradual changes, as small steps. Here the analytical relationship plays a very decisive part—at least for those schools that adhere to depth-psychology. No less important is the behavior of the analyst with respect to his or her ability to sense when the level of optimal emotional stress on the client has been reached.

Now I will briefly describe how I handled the dream narrated above (p. 100), along with the consequences of my approach. To begin with, the analysand gave me no interpretive perspective whatsoever. He did not enter more deeply into any of the dream's details. He only looked at me very expectantly. No doubt quite irritated by his unspoken "Now *you* do something," I referred directly to the shadow figure. "So when do you feel like this guy?" I asked him.

"Guy" (*Typ*) was the word he had used when recounting the dream. I took up the word, as it was clear to me that it can be a complex-laden word. "You think I rape young girls!" he burst out. "I suppose you think I am the fiend they are looking for that has been abducting girls lately. . . ." And he went on in this vein.

He became terribly abusive, stood up, paced the room in circles: a real crisis caught hold of him. Then he began crying and sat down again. I said to him, "You are defending yourself against this man, and yet he appears in your own dreams."

My first question was strongly conflict-oriented. This was no doubt in part a defense against my own irritation, which I might have addressed in a better way. Thus I next referred to the defense in the form in which it appeared in the dream. At this he breathed a sigh of relief, but repeated it could still be that I would think such a thing of him, and so on. I replied that I understood what a great conflict existed for him between his conscious self-image and the shadow side of his personality, embodied in this man. It was understandable that he would defend himself against it, and that he would defend himself against my identifying him with this figure.

My interpretation was aimed at pointing out the discrepancy between his ego and this shadow figure. I was helping him to stop the total identification with the shadow figure toward which he was tending at the moment. At the same time, I was carefully suggesting that his idea of my catching him "in the act" by means of this identification might be his own projection, thus also supporting him in his defensive behavior.

"Yes, but you know," he responded, "this conceited guy, he's not so completely strange to me. I even have a thick, gold chain."

Initially the conflict-centered interpretation precipitated a vigorous crisis. In retrospect, this crisis also facilitated a great deal of memory work. Since his youth, this shadow side of his was accosted again and again. At first he had flirted with it, but later he reacted against it in a very exaggerated way. Behind this form of reaction was his tendency to identify himself with the shadow side of his personality, and then, as a result of a radically altered self-image, to become frightened and to distance himself again from it.

I have included this example in order to show how easily a therapeutic process can get into a crisis. Such a crisis can be highly meaningful therapeutically or, under other circumstances, less meaningful.

Whether a crisis enters into a therapy, and the degree to which this is experienced as meaningful, depends on three areas of psychic activity. The first is the area of defense, coping, and compensation mechanisms. The second is that of emotions, fantasies, and drives constellated in the unconscious. The third, extremely important area is the analytic relationship between analyst and analysand.

A crisis can arise when a complex, constellated with a great deal of energy, suddenly possesses an overriding force. This happened, for example, in the falling-in-love crisis treated as an example of a crisis of overstimulation in Chapter Three.

A crisis can also arise when analysand and analyst—perhaps in concert—engage in defense. I would like to take up this problem again in greater depth by discussing a "creeping" crisis within a therapeutic process, for we are concerned here with highly complicated processes. When a problem is constellated that is uncomfortable not only for the analysand but also for the analyst, it can precipitate a strenuous defense on the part of both parties. As a result the problem becomes more urgent and virulent. A creative crisis can develop out of this if the problem comes to the consciousness of both parties.

The most important triggers for crises in the therapeutic process, however, are problems in the relationship between analyst and analysand.

Provoking a Crisis

Should it appear therapeutically necessary to provoke a crisis, any one of the three areas mentioned above can be used as a starting point.

Ciompi describes a therapeutic approach which he calls "the technique of the provoked crisis."[3] It is based on the findings of Lindemann and Caplan to the effect that a labile phase sets in at the peak of a crisis which allows new patterns of behavior to be learned with unusual ease.[4] Psychophysiological stress climbs until it reaches a point at which old ways can be dispensed with and new ones become possible.

Ciompi reports on using the technique of provoked crisis with chronic patients. He mentions one patient who had settled in on a certain ward. She was very anxious and would not leave this ward, taking on a lot of chores and becoming highly prized there. The problem was that she could not leave the ward even long enough to have dental work done, for example. After all other attempts had failed to get her out of the ward, the team decided to provoke crisis, which ran as follows. She was transferred to another ward, and the work with which she was familiar and which gave her recognition was taken away. She went into an anxious-depressive crisis for which she immediately received behavioral therapy. She was forced into a massive confrontation with her anxiety. Even her teeth were repaired, with her consent. By means of this provoked crisis, she became acquainted with a new assortment of behavioral possibilities. New modes of experience became accessible to her as well. After getting the crisis under control, she was able to live in a pension, to work as a nurse's aid in a home for the elderly, and to move about on her own. The crisis brought her old behavioral pattern to a standstill; it connected her with people who supported her and who demonstrated by their intervention that they believed that more was possible for her in life; and it brought her into contact with new life potential. Ciompi apologizes for this manipulative technique, which, by the way, he imagines could also be put to use in politics.

However, I do not believe that one can arbitrarily provoke crises. A crisis has its time, and *at that time* there is a high probability that one can provoke it. It can be inferred from Ciompi's approach that the provoked crisis comes about when the attending team enters into its own crisis with the patient.

A crisis can take the place of motivation which has been either missing or insufficient. In the crisis interventions discussed in the previous chapters, we were dealing primarily with stormy emotions and constellated complexes. One hardly needed a magnifying glass to see them in living color; they were emotionally distinct. There was pressure caused by suffering. Motivation for self-confrontation and the pressure of suffering are equivalent in many ways. Of course, psychological stress is not the only kind of stress that precipitates crises. Physical illness, for example, can also put us under enormous stress, as can problems in our social environment.

There are some therapies that place little emphasis on emotions. As an analyst, I have the feeling that little happens in these therapies, or at most, that the same thing happens over and over. The suspicion grows that persons come to these therapies to ventilate and then go again without much of anything decisively changing. The analysand "chit chats," and therapists find themselves beginning to chit chat along with them. Should something not be *done* for a change, some resolutions made? Yet we remain uncertain as to whether the analysand might need more time, or wonder whether we are simply impatient. Increasingly such therapists fall into their own crises, crises that strike at their professional self-images. They ask themselves what they are actually doing. Is it really still therapy? They tell themselves that they are letting themselves be used for something they don't like at all, and they reach a point when they have had enough.

Let us say a therapist has decided one morning, before seeing anyone, that it just can't go on like this any longer. He or she will then work in a markedly less defense-centered way, and in a much more conflict-centered way, than usual. The heat is on the analysand, who senses the therapist's resolve to instigate a change, which can be experienced as a withdrawal of love. This situation could be seen as the point of departure for a deliberately provoked crisis. If, after having worked for a long time in a defense-centered mode—as a "nice therapist" until now—the therapist suddenly begins to work in a conflict-centered way, new energy is sparked. This naturally creates new problems for the therapeutic relationship. The situation should not yet be called a provoked crisis, but a crisis can arise out of such a situation. If it does, it must be handled very consciously and responsibly.

For example, a forty-eight-year-old painter, whose main problems in life were alcohol and relationships, would not let go of his twenty-three-year-old daughter. He declared her his muse. He manipulated her by telling her that if she moved out, he would lose his inspiration. He also had problems with his artistic creativity.

We began working together therapeutically. An alcohol-withdrawal treatment was in fact needed, but the analysand was not quite a habitual drinker, only a nearly habitual drinker, with period bouts of severity. Every time he finished another heavy drinking episode, he would announce that he really should submit himself to a withdrawal treatment. But then, usually in the same breath, he would remark that things were going rather well now; he could paint again; it was not an advantageous time for a treatment. No time seemed to suit him.

At the beginning of our work together, he suddenly began getting a lot of new ideas about how and what he could paint. He talked at length about these ideas. But he only turned a few of them into reality, because he was "so absorbed by duties." We attempted to sort out these duties. We even engaged public services to help get them in order. He gave exhibits, and we worked on problems arising in connection with those.

For a long period of time he consistently spoke with great enthusiasm in the analytical sessions about his paintings, and impatience mounted within me. I did find the discussions quite stimulating. At the end of the hour, we would sit looking at the pile of sketches he had made during the session. A creative atmosphere prevailed, an atmosphere of plans being made, of castles being built in the air. I couldn't completely resist the magic of this atmosphere. At the same time, it made me uneasy to think of the many problems he had that we should be pursuing. After a while I began to request twenty minutes from every hour to discuss problems. This ran rather stereotypically: he confessed to having problems with alcohol, with his wife, with his daughter, with money, etc. Yet he repeatedly concluded that either nothing was *really* wrong, or else everything was *so* wrong that it could not be dealt with in therapy. The problems he described repeated themselves, and slowly they became—like his sketches on the floor—more and more boring. He would tell me that he had dreamt, but had forgotten what about. At the beginning of the analysis, he had painted his dreams with interpenetrating colors, and he would relate these colors to the various emotional nuances of his dreams. Eventually even these painted dreams stopped appearing.

I grew more and more restless and dissatisfied, until I reached the point of feeling I would have to do something. Then one day I caught myself wishing a crisis on him, and right around the same time, two crucial events occurred. The analysand, com-pletely drunk, had an accident with his moped: he drove into a wall. The accident prevented him from playing tennis, from going hiking, and from mountain climbing. Tennis had been an especially important way for him to compensate. It gave him the chance to meet interesting women, and being a good, enthusiastic tennis partner, he could be something of a hero on the court. Hiking was also important because it gave him the feeling of getting in touch with himself. Together, these two compensatory activities guaranteed him adequate self-esteem. Both were taken away as a result of the accident. In addition, his daughter left for western Switzerland to complete an urgently required internship.

Like a storm on the horizon, the crisis gathered. He reported all of these problems to me in the analytical hour, adding that it was really difficult for him at the moment to limit his drinking to the amount on which we had agreed. He needed to drink now in order to cope with the situation, and must have hoped I would go along with this. Sensing that the decisive crisis in the therapeutic process was in the air, I instead thought about how I might be able to give it an extra push to get it started or give it more power. Although he was under considerable pressure, it nonetheless seemed to me insufficient in light of his hope to master this crisis with alcohol. I was aware that pressure from his social environment was mounting as well: his wife had renewed her announcement that her patience was exhausted.

I told him I could well understand how he might regard alcohol more now than ever as a way to cope with his problems, but that I didn't see how we could continue our therapeutic work together under such circumstances. I placed my faith in our relationship, deliberately putting it on the line to challenge him, since it was relatively good and of some importance to him.

"Since drying out is unthinkable at the moment," I added, "it would be meaningless for us to continue to work at the same pace, an hour per week." I suggested that from now on he come for an hour once every three weeks. After drying out, if that were possible, I would anticipate a creative crisis, in which case I would be prepared to see him two hours a week. He listened to me in a friendly mood—heavily under the influence of alcohol—and took my suggestion with perfect detachment, as if to say, "Whatever you think; you know better than I."

I was not nearly as comfortable with the whole matter as he. On the one hand, it was important to me that this man experience a decisive crisis. On the other hand, I was worried about manipulating him too much.

Late that same evening, his wife telephoned. He was dead drunk, she had called in a social worker, and they were both in favor of taking him to the hospital to undergo a withdrawal treatment. The plan was carried out.

I visited him three days after his admittance to the hospital, and he unambiguously stated his desire to dry up. Looking back on our last talk, he admitted how wretched he had felt. He felt as if everyone was abandoning him. No one was sticking with him, not even me, whose job it was supposed to be. Yet he also felt that something was finally happening.

To my questioning conclusion, "You must have been wonderfully angry at me," he replied, "Yes, but you know, angry that you didn't do that a long time ago."

The withdrawal treatment was then conducted, and something like a creative crisis actually did follow. It enabled him to deal with many issues, and he experienced a real spurt of growth, which could be seen in his paintings. His relationship to his daughter and to his wife changed visibly. Some time later, the therapeutic process fell into a rut once more, congruent with his character. We very seriously considered whether and how we should provoke another crisis. This time, the crisis came from outside, in the form of a tax bill, just as he was setting up an important exhibition. This crisis was substantially less creative.

A provoked crisis can bring on a spurt of growth, but it is no cure-all; with some persons, this process comes to a dead end again and again. This is easier to accept if we do not bind ourselves too rigidly to an ethic of individuation.

Naturally it is important to be very conscious of why one, as a therapist is provoking a crisis and to be convinced that it is meaningful. A crisis will always have dimensions we have not anticipated and could not have seen in advance. It is crucial to be available during a provoked crisis and to be prepared if necessary to carry out a plan of action that is considerably more extended than normal, both temporally and emotionally.

Concealed Crises

There are also crises that silently and stealthily creep into the therapeutic process. This can happen in analyses that are proceeding well enough, for a given analysis need not be better than good enough. I repeatedly meet with the expectation that something most unusual must be happening constantly in analysis, which is of course not the reality. Analytical reports do not exactly discourage this: a concentrated bundle of essentials is presented, while the quiet process of maturation over time eludes adequate representation. There are analyses that open with a stormy peak of personality growth and then flatten out over a long period of time, during which many things in the analysand's life become clear. In the report of such a case, the plateau may be described with a few sentences. It is not necessary for analysis to be a nonstop thriller. I consider an analysis good enough when analyst and analysand sense each other's understandings and misunderstandings, when they are able to talk about them, when now and then a "little light goes on," when an image takes hold and engrosses one deeply so that life takes on a new shape.

Such analyses, which are experienced by both parties as good enough, can become the victim of a concealed crisis. Suddenly the analysis becomes problematic and tiresome. Without really knowing why, one has the feeling that everything flowed much better before and was more interesting. Now the situation has become bland somehow. Problems continue to be formulated and understood, or at least, it is assumed that they are understood. One interprets them, understood or not, but the interpretations suddenly cease to function, at least not as they did before. This is how one gets entangled in a concealed crisis.

For example, a woman between thirty-five and forty years of age came for therapy with the diagnosis of exhaustion depression. She was suffering from relationship problems, which she described with the sentence, "I am only loved when I do everything for others."

With her oldest children leaving home, her life situation was becoming difficult. We started out by working on the experience of loss, which went well. Basically, the theme of individuation, appropriate to this time of life, was thrusting into the foreground such questions as: Who am I? What do I want? What do I still want to do with my life? She was trying to find a new form of relationship with her husband. He had a similar need: life, which until now had been centered around the children, began looking very different to him, too. The analysand brought in dreams, not in overabundance but every now and then, usually when it was important for the therapy to receive guidance from the unconscious. She developed a good understanding of dreams within a period of about a year. Thus it was basically a therapy that was going along just fine, or so I imagined. Then we entered into a phase in which I had the impression that the therapy was somehow slipping away from me. I wondered whether it might not be time to bring the analysis slowly to a close. During this phase, the analysand said to me that she felt as though I was no longer very interested in her, as though I found her a bore.

I reflected on whether my interest had indeed dwindled. I realized that she was, in fact, now leading a substantially more interesting life than before and that her main problems had been reduced in magnitude. I told her I did not have the sense of being less interested in her now than in the past. I was, however, less worried about her now than at the beginning of the analysis; I had the feeling that she had become quite autonomous and could now cope with a lot on her own. It was conceivable that our analysis was drawing slowly to a close. She listened to me and then exclaimed that she did not want to stop the analysis and that I must really find her a bore.

There was a childhood trauma that we had often singled out as an important theme: her father had constantly remarked that, unfortunately, he had had only daughters—six of them—and that daughters were boring. As a child, she had always made an effort to be the way her father wanted her to be, to avoid receiving the stamp of "bore." This must have been the origin of the sentence, "I am only loved when I do everything for others." She had periodically succeeded in winning her father's attention, only to hear him invariably saying to others later, "Unfortunately I have only daughters; daughters are boring." Moreover, the mother did not come to the aid of her daughters. Apparently she accepted this deprecation, no doubt on account of her own guilt feelings over having borne her husband only daughters, not to mention her own sense of unworthiness.

I was convinced that a situation requiring detachment from the therapy and from me was imminent, and that she was still in the phase of denying this. I wondered whether she had also thought about ending the analysis, and whether, because of guilt feelings, she was defending herself against this thought. Further, I suspected that she was transferring her childhood relationship to her father onto the analytical relationship; now she would be trying to find out what she must do to avoid boring me. To begin with, I planned to have a discussion on the theme of her low self-esteem in the face of a father who had not accepted her. In this connection, we would discuss her inhibited aggression, her feeling of not being able to do what she really wanted to do, and her experience of me—on account of this situation—as a rejecting father.

I attempted to get this interpretation across to her. On the one hand, it stimulated a lot of memories. She recounted many stories of how she used to set about doing something with her father. He would assure her that she could practically replace the son for whom he longed. But when she joined her girlfriends again, she unfortunately became a girl again and, like all girls, boring. Quite a bit of distressing material came to light. She then told me how in relation to her daughter, who was in the process of detaching herself, she was taking a position similar to the position that I, the analyst, was taking in relation to her, the analysand: she felt less worried about her daughter, but had also lost some of her interest in her. I could see that she was identifying with her daughter, but I kept asking myself whether this "having less interest" was not a projection, an attempt to force detachment by withdrawing interest from the analogous person, in this case me. I tried to make all of this, and much more, understandable to her, without success. Time after time she came to the hour with the remark, "I just have the feeling we cannot work with each other anymore; you find me a bore!" Moreover, she reported that although she didn't much like coming any more, she still didn't want to quit. After a while, I found this unceasing lament about her boringness increasingly boring; I really did get bored. There were no more interpretations I could offer to sustain my active role in the therapy. Nothing more occurred to me; I was out of things to say. I had the feeling that she was blaming me for the stagnation of our process; that nothing was happening anymore because I found her boring. I would not accept this blame because I felt that it did not correspond to the reality of the situation. But I became increasingly angry as her prophecy fulfilled itself and the situation became incredibly tiresome. I found her stubbornly insisting that she bored me, and I found myself stubbornly insisting that she should set the problem of boredom aside once and for all. I was angry with myself for not being able to handle the problem more gracefully. I was angry that I could not come up with anything else, that I had gotten so stuck in a rut.

Having admitted to myself how terribly angry I was, with my analysand sitting there before me again, I thought there must be some solution. I left her accusation hanging for the moment and turned my attention to myself. I asked myself what was wrong with me. I searched for an inner image, concentrating on what it might be able to say in a symbolic way about the problem that had been touched off in me. No images appeared, but I did suddenly hear the sentence, "Boring people must die." This sentence gave me an enormous shock. Did I have a death wish against this woman on the grounds of such a triviality? The idea that I could have a death wish for my analysand was hardly compatible with my analytical self-image. It offended me; I was horrified, upset, and amazed by the sentence I had heard. It suddenly occurred to me that I could react in exactly the same way as her father, for his statement, "You are a girl and girls are boring," basically contained a death wish as well. Suddenly I understood what it was that I hadn't been able to accept: I did not want to be as brutal as her father. I did not want to assume the father image that she had been projecting onto me. Instead, I wanted to take care of the problem of boredom once and for all at the level of interpretation, because the feelings associated with it disturbed me deeply. For me, they contained a death wish.

Thus I understood the sentence, "Boring people must die," as a threat to both of us. It was the threat of an incredibly destructive power, capable of denying another person's right to exist, capable even of denying one's own right to exist, should one be boring. It was a destructiveness that could also be hiding within both of us.

I shared my insight with her by saying, "But even if we do bore each other, that is no reason for us to die."

While I was asking myself if that was really an adequate intervention, she suddenly looked at me, relieved, and said, "You have finally comprehended how unbelievably dangerous it is to be a bore."

She understood me perfectly, although I couldn't tell whether she had followed the entire process that had gone on within me. I didn't repeat the sentence to her exactly as I had heard it, but rather my version of it: my refusal to let anyone be killed because of boredom. This enabled the analysand to bring to expression not only the total threat of annihilation posed by boredom, but also the entire brutality that she had felt from her father. I had felt this brutality in myself for a moment.

I experience extreme difficulty with therapeutic situations in which archaic destructiveness, archaic rage, and archaic anxiety suddenly make themselves felt, in both myself and my analysand. Thus I can understand why I defended myself for so long against the feelings of brutality. This seems to me an aspect of the therapeutic profession to which we pay too little attention. Not only are personal relationships from the analysand's past transferred onto the analyst, along with the underlying archetypal constellations that give these relationships their emotional tone; also transferred are the associated emotions that we as therapists then experience as both our own and yet the same time not our own. Clearly the transference can activate conflictual relationships in one's personal unconscious. But in addition, emotions are activated that have to do with our collective history as human beings, beyond our individual life histories. Of course, we also mobilize resistances against these threatening emotions.[5] In my opinion, a great deal of defensive behavior on the part of therapists has to do with archaic feelings coming alive, feelings that we never confronted in our own analyses, simply because no one had awakened them in us.

With her problem, this analysand had called up in me the problem of being threatened with death through boredom. To begin with, I dealt with it by means of the defense mechanism of intellectualization. I believe that this defense prevented us from finding contact with each other, since both of us loss contact with ourselves in these sessions.[6] Our relationship ran astray and the tension mounted, paving the way for a crisis. Crisis intervention became possible when I stopped stubbornly expecting her to put away her boring problem of being a bore. It began when I found an empathic relationship to myself, when I asked myself—empathically instead of angrily—what was actually wrong with me. By devoting this kind of attention to myself, and by deliberately waiting for an image, I was able to neutralize my rigid defense. I was able to see that my defense had denied the analysand the possibility of perceiving, in herself and in myself, this absolute threat to life, evidently triggered by the theme of boredom. This made it imperative for me to admit—if only for an instant— the impulse of the sadistic father, which I so rejected.

Anxiety can only be coped with when both defense and anxiety are experienced by the same person, in a single psyche. Here, they were split: I, the therapist, took the part of defense, while the analysand took the part of anxiety. She tortured me with this anxiety, constantly bringing it back into the therapy, but I would not listen. Only when we could look together at what was being defended against could the therapeutic process once again proceed satisfactorily.

I believe that we are dealing here with very complicated processes and that this form of crisis must be handled with extreme care. It is not always easy for therapists to accept what the transference animates in them, even when it is only temporary.

Concluding Remarks

Crisis intervention is called for when one's existence is seized by a crisis. No other depth-psychological technique can substitute for it.

It is in the nature of a crisis—the way it narrows life and brings it to a head—to prepare the ground for a breakthrough. New possibilities for living and new qualities of experience come within reach and reveal themselves. Or the crisis can end in a breakdown. Even death may be sought as the way out.

Since the distress of this emotional situation "concentrates" life on a primary problem that carries with it both an inhibitory and a developmental theme, one experiences the life issue standing in need of attention and calling for integration, together with associated problems, in a less disguised form than is characteristic of less stressful situations. A crisis thus facilitates the therapist's cognitive and emotional grasp of the problematic themes. This is the great advantage of crisis intervention. The major disadvantage is the extreme anxiety associated with a crisis, which can hinder all who are involved and blind them to the obvious.

A crisis intervention's success depends on how those involved deal with the situation's pervading anxiety. This determines whether the intervention can give an individual some distance from his or her crisis. Can that individual elude his or her bondage to the crisis in order to establish a relationship with it? Can the impulse for development be received and cultivated? In the final analysis, this creative drive toward growth is the cause of the crisis (except with crises of loss, strictly defined). But the success of the intervention also depends on whether helping persons manage to establish contact with persons in crisis. The latter make contact with their crises by making contact with another person. Insofar as they dare to open up to another, it is possible, step by step, to reverse the narrowing trend so that the potential for growth that is pushing its way into life through the crisis may be born.

Indeed, when a crisis becomes unbearable, the fact that someone feels compelled to seek help is already a sign that hope for contact and openness to it already exist. Those who are beyond the point of putting their hope in a relationship, or who remain stubbornly certain that each individual must solve his or her problems without the help of others, are hardly suitable candidates for a crisis intervention. Of such persons we know little—only that there are many of them.

Establishing contact with someone in crisis hinges more on the crisis than on the person. It is made easier if the therapist can quickly sense and express the feelings of the person in crisis. The dynamics of the crisis itself greatly facilitate this. Quick comprehension of the relevant problems and emotions at the beginning of a crisis intervention may at times sound like magic. But it is really a matter of perceiving the nuances of the relational dynamic and of the feelings triggered within oneself, for one's own feelings often accurately reflect those of the person in crisis. The facility of this mirroring is caused above all by the dynamic of the crisis. Our own feelings, triggered by the crisis, are able to mirror those of the person in crisis because the latter are strong and, less altered by defense, affect us on the emotional level as we concentrate ourselves fully on the crisis.

Therapists must naturally concern themselves with the feelings that are awakened in them through contact with the crisis. They must look at how the therapeutic relationship is constellated, noticing its peculiar features and emotional nuances. If they can find a suitable moment to convey all of this in the form of a cautious interpretation that explains the affected person's difficulties, he or she will feel understood. Anxiety is then reduced, and new coping mechanisms can be deployed.

Persons undergoing a crisis must quickly get the feeling that their unbearable situation is understood. And they must be able to trust the person helping them. The therapist must be someone with whom they can walk this tightrope. Crisis intervention is a tightrope walk *par excellence*: either the crisis is delivered safely to the other side, or else the person in crisis tumbles down the line of social agencies. An unsuccessful intervention may be linked to a loss of hope. Or the intensity of a crisis may subside before one has really succeeded in grasping the developmental issue at hand.

I have witnessed the failure of crisis interventions in cases where an issue of personal growth was thoroughly grasped, strategies were discovered for dealing with the everyday problems involved, and yet the issue could not be carried over into the practice of life. In a crisis intervention, as in the creative process, the issue must be brought into life and tried out there. The newly discovered strategies must be put to work. New ways of behaving must be risked. This does not always happen. Many persons come to a crisis intervention with the plea, "Help me get back to the way I was." Once the emotional intensity of this exceptional situation has died down and they are back to "the way they were"—at least as far as their emotional equilibrium is concerned—they no longer see any reason to concern themselves with their crisis. In such cases the person does not seem to take advantage of the potential for growth contained in the crisis to any great extent. I make this statement with a certain reserve, because it is extremely difficult to judge whether the person has taken advantage of an impulse for development or not. Sometimes it is taken up in a way that we simply cannot see.

Furthermore, the inability to act on many of the impulses that come our way seems very much in accord with the nature of the human creature. Even so, the call of life goes out to us with a certain persistence in the form of crises. Our crises beckon us to open ourselves again, to reorient ourselves among our inner possibilities so that our competence to solve outer problems may grow. Only seldom can we open ourselves in the absence of others who allow themselves to be touched by the crisis. Crisis situations begin to see the light of day when we unlock our inner chambers in relationship with another human being.

Notes

Introduction

1. See P. Heimann, "Bemerkungen zur Gegenübertragung," *Psyche* 18 (1964):483–493.
2. M. Ermann, "Die Gegenübertragung und die Widestaude des Psychoanalytikes," *Forum Psychoanal.* 2 (1987):103–113.
3. J. Sandler, "Gegenübertragung und Rollenübernahme," *Psyche* 4 (1976):297–305.
4. C. G. Jung, "The Psychology of the Transference," *The Practice of Psychology*, CW 16 (Princeton, N.J.: Princeton University Press, 1954), pp. 163–323; J. Sandler, "Gegenübertragung."

Chapter One

1. G. Caplan, *Principles of Preventive Psychiatry* (London: Tavistock Publications, 1964).
2. K. Jaspers, *General Psychopathology* (Chicago: University of Chicago Press, 1963), p. 698.
3. See E. Landau, *Kreatives Erleben* (Munich: Reinhardt, 1984).

Chapter Three

1. V. Kast, *The Nature of Loving: Patterns of Human Relationship*, Boris Matthews, trans. (Wilmette, Ill.: Chiron Publications, 1986).
2. E. Ringel, *Selbstmordverhütung* (Bern: Huber, 1969, 1984).

Chapter Four

1. James Hillman, *Suicide and the Soul* (New York: Spring, 1976).
2. W. Pöldinger and M. Stoll-Hürliman, *Krisenintervention auf interdisziplinärer Basis* (Bern: Huber, 1980).
3. C. H. Reimer and H. Henseler, *Selbstmordgefährdung*, Problemata (Stuttgart: Frommann-Holzboog, 1981).
4. J. Amery, *Hand an sich legen: Diskurs über den Freitod* (Stuttgart: Klett-Cotta, 1976).
5. Hillman, *Suicide and the Soul.*
6. C. G. Jung, *Letters*, vol. 1 (Princeton, N.J.: Princeton University Press, 1973), p. 434.
7. Ibid., p. 436
8. A. Leutwiler, "Über den Umgang mit Suizidgefährdeten," in *Kurzpsychotherapie und Krisenintervention*, P. M. Pflüger, ed. (Fellbach: Bonz, 1978), p. 199ff.
9. H. Henseler, *Narzißtische Krisen: Zur Psychodynamik des Selbstmords* (Hamburg: Rowohlt, Studium rororo 58, 1974).
10. Ringel, *Selbstmordverhütung.*
11. See K. Asper, *Verlassenheit und Selbstentfremdung* (Olten: Walter, 1987).

12. Ringel, *Selbstmordverhütung.*
13. Henseler, *Narzißtische Krisen.*
14. I. Koppány, "Zur Frage der Objektbeziehungen und des Selbstkonzeptes bei Suizidanten," in C. H. Reimer and H. Henseler, *Selbstmordgefährdung* (Stuttgart: Frommann-Holzboog, 1981), p. 55ff; H. Phillipson, *Object Relations Technique* (London: NFER Publishing Co. Ltd., 1973).
15. See Reimer and Henseler, *Selbstmordgefährdung.*
16. V. Kast, *Imagination als Raum der Freiheit* (Olten: Walter, 1988).
17. Henseler, *Narzißtische Krisen.*
18. M. Hefti, "Selbstmord: Ein menschliches Phänomen," dissertation for the University of Zurich, 1986.

Chapter Five

1. V. Kast, *A Time to Mourn: Growing through the Grief Process,* Diana Dachler and Fiona Cairns, trans. (Einsiedeln, Switzerland: Daimon, 1988).
2. E. Lindemann, *Jenseits von Trauer* (Göttingen: Vandenhoeck and Ruprecht, 1985).
3. E. Kübler-Ross, *Interviews mit Sterbenden* (Stuttgart: Kreuz Verlag, 1980). Kübler-Ross describes five phases an individual goes through upon learning that he suffers from a terminal illness:
   1st Phase: Denial and isolation
   2nd Phase: Anger
   3rd Phase: Bargaining
   4th Phase: Depression
   5th Phase: Acceptance
   Kübler-Ross describes the phase of depression thus: the individual takes leave and mourns, because he must take leave of so many. These stages described by Kübler-Ross seem to me also to apply to the process of mourning undergone by those left behind.
4. Kast, *The Nature of Loving.*

Chapter Six

1. T. von Uexküll and W. Wesiack, "Wissenschaftstheorie und psychosomatische Medizin, ein biopsycho-soziales Modell," in *Psychosomatische Medizin,* Rolf Adler, ed. (Schwarzenberg: von Uexküll, 1986).
2. D. Beck, "Krankheit als Selbstheilung," *Suhrkamp Taschenb.* 1126 (1985); F. Capra, *Wendezeit* (Bern: Scherz-Verlag, 1983); E. Overbeck, "Krankheit als Anpassung. Der Sozio-psychosomatische Zirkel," *Suhrkamp Taschenb.* 973 (1984); H. H. Studt, ed., *Psychosomatik in Forschung und Praxis* (Schwarzenberg: Baltiwor, 1983); T. Stuttgen, *Interaktionelle Psychosomatik* (Berlin: Springer, 1985).
3. See H. Dieckmann, "Die libidinöse Wiederbesetzung des Körpers in der Psychosomatik," *Zeitschrift für Analytische Psychologie* 12 (1981), p. 268ff.
4. Kast, *Imagination.*
5. E. Wiesenhütter, *Blick nach drüben* (Gütersloh: GTB 196, 1976).

6. H. G. Rechenberger, "Was ist Kurztherapie?" in *Kurzpsychotherapie*, P. M. Pfluger, ed. (Fellbach: Bonz, 1978); D. Beck, *Die Kurzpsychotherapie* (Bern: Huber, 1974).

7. D. H. Malan, *Psychoanalytische Kurztherapie* (Stuttgart: Huber/Klett, 1962).

8. P. Fürstenau, *Zur Theorie psychoanalytischer Praxis* (Stuttgart: Klett-Cotta, 1979).

Chapter Seven

1. J. Willi, *Die Zweierbeziehung* (Hamburg: Rowohlt, 1975.)

Chapter Eight

1. V. Kast, *Das Assoziationsexperiment in der therapeutischen Praxis* (Fellbach: Bonz, 1980).

2. J. Franck, "Les facteurs curatifs des psychothérapies," in Ciompi, *Gedanken zu den therapeutischen Möglichkeiten einer Technik der provozierten Krise*, Psychiatrica clin. 10 (1977).

3. Ciompi, *Gedanken zu den Möglichkeiten.*

4. Lindemann, *Jenseits von Trauer*; Caplan, *Preventive Psychiatry.*

5. Jung, "Psychology of the Transference," pp. 186–189. See also Ermann, "Die Gegenübertragung."

6. See Ermann, "Die Gegenübertragung."

Index

Other titles by Chiron Publications

Verena Kast
The Nature of Loving: Patterns of Human Relationship
107 pages   86–063   (paper) $12.95

Peter Schellenbaum
How to Say No to the One You Love:
The Role of Boundaries in Human Relationships
137 pages   87–25X   (cloth) $16.95

Maud Oakes
The Stone Speaks: The Memoir of a Personal Transformation
148 pages   87–047   (paper) $12.95
87–233   (cloth) $24.95

Theodor Seifert
Snow White: Life Almost Lost
131 pages   86–08X   (paper) $10.95

Allan B. Chinen
In the Ever After: Fairy Tales and the Second Half of Life
216 pages   89–411   (paper) $14.95

Barbara Stevens Sullivan
Psychotherapy Grounded in the Feminine Principle
224 pages   89–438   (paper) $16.95

Eugene T. Gendlin
Let Your Body Interpret Your Dreams
195 pages   86-012   (paper) $14.95

Harry A. Wilmer, ed.
Mother Father
208 pages   90–454   (paper) $14.95

Edward F. Edinger
The Living Psyche: A Jungian Analysis in Pictures
232 pages   89–527   (paper) $19.95

Russell A. Lockhart
Psyche Speaks: A Jungian Approach to Self and World
130 pages   87–225   (paper) $12.95
87–284   (cloth) $19.95

To order, write or call Chiron Publications, 400 Linden Avenue, Wilmette, Illinois
60091. (708) 256-7551, (800) 397-8109, fax (708) 256-2202.